SMART PEOPLE

SMART PEOPLE

≈ A PLAY ≈

LYDIA R. DIAMOND

NORTHWESTERN UNIVERSITY PRESS

EVANSTON, ILLINOIS

Northwestern University Press
www.nupress.northwestern.edu

Printed in the United States of America

10 9 8 7 6 5 4 3 2 1

ISBN 978-0-8101-3464-5 [paper]
ISBN 978-0-8101-3465-2 [e-book]

LIBRARY OF CONGRESS
CATALOGING-IN-PUBLICATION DATA

Names: Diamond, Lydia R., 1969– author.
Title: Smart people : a play / Lydia R. Diamond.
Description: Evanston, Illinois : Northwestern University Press, 2016.
Identifiers: LCCN 2016044885 | ISBN 9780810134645 (pbk. : alk paper) | ISBN 9780810134652 (e-book)
Classification: LCC PS3604.I1557 S63 2016 | DDC 812/.6—dc23
LC record available at https://lccn.loc.gov/2016044885

To Baylor and John

CONTENTS

ACKNOWLEDGMENTS

So many people to thank. Over the course of the seven years it has taken me to write this, countless artists have contributed their time, talents, and intellect to bring this baby home. I could not possibly include all of the actors who have embodied these characters in countless readings, workshops, and productions. Suffice to say . . . You're all in there . . . a little bit of you in all of these characters that I love so much. Interns, literary staff, stage managers, directors, friends, family . . . if I've left you off, and most certainly I will have excluded some of the most integral players . . . please know that I love you, and chalk it up to ADD. But here are some names . . . of some of the most consistent players: Emily Mann, Mara Isaacs, Carrie Hughes, Adam Immerwahr, Emilia LaPenta, and the whole McCarter family . . . thank you for commissioning this play and providing constant support. Peter DuBois—you made it happen. Twice. Thank you for your ridiculous amount of talent. Thank you for getting it, and championing it, and producing it, and directing it with such a deft hand. Thank you for being my friend. Charles Haughland, Lisa Timmel, Michael Maso, and all of you Huntington people, you just could not have supported me more through the years. Summer Williams, Ilana Brownstein, Shawn LaCount, and the whole Company One family, thank you for workshopping this play at a very critical stage. The Radcliffe Institute, Daisy Hay, Katherine Ibbett, Tstitsi Jaji, Jane Rhodes, Carole Rothman, Chris Burney—Second Stage family, a second production wow . . . America needs more of those. Kenny Leon—we did it again, and I am so proud and grateful for you as a true friend and brilliant colleague. And now I'm listing . . . You all know what you did, and the thank-yous extend to the people who surround and support you as you supported me: Jocelyn Clarke, True Colors, Chuck Smith, Russ Tutterow, Chicago Dramatists, Kwame Kwei-Armah, Gavin Witt, Centerstage, Jim Petosa, Beverly Morgan-Welch, Monica White Ndounou, Nicole Salter,

Jenny Ikeda, University of Wisconsin and all of the lovely actors and designers who made that production happen, Amy Click, Emily Click, Bruce Ostler, Michael L. Levine, and all of the people at Northwestern University Press who have patience with me . . . slowest person ever to turn around a galley. Christine Velez (Baylor's first love), Josefa Velez, Rayan Elkheir, and all of the other incredible women who took care of Baylor when I couldn't. Last but not least, Baylor Diamond, John Diamond who helped make Baylor and supported me and my work for more than twenty-five years, Beverly Holmes, Aunt Karen, Uncle Gilbert, Uncle John, Marsha Estell, Deidre Searcy-Long, Michelle Wilson, Penelope Walker, Mignon McPhearson, Alysha Hearn, my front line. Dr. Henry Perkins. Dr. James Leone. And a special thank-you to Derek Zasky, my incredible agent.

PRODUCTION HISTORY

Smart People was originally produced by the Huntington Theatre Company in Boston in 2014. Peter DuBois was the artistic director and Michael Maso was the managing director. The play was directed by Peter DuBois, with scenic design by Alexander Dodge, costume design by Junghyun Georgia Lee, lighting design by Paul Gallo, sound design by M. L. Dogg, and projection design by Aaron Rhyme. The play was originally commissioned by McCarter Theatre in Princeton, New Jersey, with Emily Mann as artistic director and Jeffrey Woodward as the managing director.

The cast of the Huntington Theatre Company production was as follows:

Valerie Johnston	Miranda Craigwell
Brian White	Roderick Hill
Ginny Yang	Eunice Wong
Jackson Moore	McKinley Belcher III

The New York premiere of *Smart People* was produced by Second Stage Theatre in 2016. Carole Rothman was the artistic director and Casey Reitz was the executive director. The play was directed by Kenny Leon, with scenic design by Riccardo Hernandez, costume design by Paul Tazewell, lighting design by Jason Lyons, sound design by Nevin Steinberg, projection design by Zachary G. Borovay, and original music by Zane Mark. The cast was as follows:

Valerie Johnston	Tessa Thompson
Brian White	Joshua Jackson
Ginny Yang	Anne Son
Jackson Moore	Mahershala Ali

Smart People was developed in part at True Colors Theatre Company in Atlanta, Georgia, and produced there in 2016. Kenny Leon was the artistic director and Jennifer McEwen was the managing director. The play was directed by David de Vries, with set design by Moriah and Isabel Curley-Clay, lighting design by Joe Futral, sound design by Kay Richardson, costume design by Shilla Benning, and projection design by Bobby Johnston. The cast was as follows:

Valerie Johnston. . . . . Danielle Deadwyler

Brian White . . . . Joe Knezevich

Ginny Yang . . . . Julee Cerda

Jackson Moore . . . . Neal Ghant

SMART PEOPLE

SETTING

Various locations in Cambridge, Massachusetts, ranging from 2007 through 2009.

CHARACTERS

Valerie Johnston, twenty-four. African American. Recently graduated A.R.T. Acting M.F.A.

Brian White, thirty-six to forty-two. White. A professor at Harvard and a neuropsychiatrist. Studies patterns of racial identity and perceptions.

Ginny Yang, thirty-four to forty. Chinese and Japanese American. No accent. Only speaks English. A respected tenured professor of psychology at Harvard. Studies race and identity among Asian American women.

Jackson Moore, twenty-eight. African American. Harvard Med School. Surgical intern on rotation.

PROLOGUE

SEPTEMBER 2007

[*Images are projected on the back wall. They change slowly, and include: A White baby in a high chair. A Pakistani woman in an expensive business suit. A little Black boy climbing on a jungle gym. A waiflike tattooed Japanese teenage girl. A Black male dancer. A White paraplegic female. A Black teenage girl wearing earbuds and dancing. An old White woman in peasant clothing. A Black man with a tweed blazer and spectacles. A White woman in formal English equestrian attire on a horse. A homeless White man . . . images continue sporadically through the scene.*]

[VALERIE *enters in leggings and a sweatshirt, rumpled script in hand. She sports very short dreadlocks. She rehearses Portia with skill and authority. It is early in the rehearsal process.*]

VALERIE:
    . . . You have ungently, Brutus,
    Stole from my bed; and yesternight, at supper,
    You suddenly arose and . . .

[*To director, who is offstage*] I have a thought . . . I've been working on Portia's backstory, and I'm thinking we can deepen her . . .

[*Apparently the director interrupts with something to the effect of, just spit the fucking words out please.*]

Oh . . . OK. Just drive it then? Sure, just plow through . . . Yeah, OK. But I . . . OK. Yes. Drive it hard.

[*Driving it hard*]

You suddenly arose and walked about,
Musing and sighing, with your arms across;
And when I ask'd you what the matter was,
You stared upon me with ungentle . . .

A five-minute break? Now? Could we just . . . OK. Five minutes. Thank you. Terrific.

[VALERIE *removes a pack of cigarettes from her pocket and exits.*]

[*Lights up on* BRIAN, *lecturing. He holds a large stack of blue books (graded tests). Even at his angriest, there is amused dedication.*]

BRIAN: Please disabuse yourselves of this notion that I am obligated to teach you. Neither do I have an obligation to bestow upon you my, and I cite *Harvard Review*, 2002, ". . . effortless charisma and probingly insightful tutelage." [*Beat.*] I am obligated only to show up and talk for two hours twice a week. Note my frustration. I am not frustrated because I see in you some sort of great, collective, untapped potential. I am frustrated because I will never have these two hours back. [*Skimming through stack*] With the exception of three outstanding students, you have all failed miserably. [*Beat.*] So. [*Reading from blue books*] Mr. Goldstein, Ms. Jones, and Mr. Shwargdagala—you have distinguished yourselves

as capable of not merely regurgitating information, but of actually absorbing and metabolizing it. You are excused from today's
lecture. [*Beat.*] Really, go! I'm giving you the day off. For being
smart. [*Beat.*] Go!

[*They're leaving; he watches them out the door.*]

Thank you.

[BRIAN *dumps the blue books into the garbage. All is forgiven.*]

So, we shall begin again? [*Beat.*]

[*Smiling*] OK, shake it off. I don't hold grudges.

[*He rolls up his sleeves and turns to the screen behind him, onto which
indecipherable charts, graphs, and matrixes are projected. Light fades.*]

[*Light rises on* GINNY, *in another area, presenting at a psychiatry
conference.*]

GINNY: Thank you for that flattering introduction, Dr. Thomason. You
all have a copy of the study, so we'll jump right in. We've inter-
viewed three hundred and fifty third-generation Asian American
women.

[*An audience member interrupts.*]

Oh . . . you have a question. Already.

[*Light rises on* JACKSON, *removing bloodied surgical gown, being
scolded by a superior.*]

JACKSON: I did not raise my voice to Dr. Sandiet [*pronounced
San-deet*] . . .

[Interrupted, apparently with "You did."]

No. No. I just pointed out the necessity of the amputation . . .

GINNY: Yes. Asian is broad. *[Beat.]* Chinese, Japanese, and Korean, it's there in your . . . Could we hold our questions until after—

[What economic bracket were they from?]

It's a good question, but if we could just—

[This person probably taught "Orientalism" in '58 and wants his moment in the sun.]

You'll see I've addressed that in . . . if we could return to . . . You. *[Pointing to him]* Stop that.

JACKSON: No. I categorically reject that. *[Beat.]* I removed the first digit on the patient's left foot.

GINNY: My findings debunk Western assumptions naming primary reasons for anxiety and depression in Asian American women as familial.

JACKSON: . . . I did ask Doctor Sandiet for permission . . . He nodded. I know what a nod is. I speak fluent gestural shorthand. I'm trying to tell you . . . damn *[interrupted]* . . .

[Somewhere through the preceding VALERIE *has returned and is back in the scene.]*

VALERIE: OK . . . so not from where we left off? Forward to where then?

JACKSON: I just need you to listen to me. Because I'm your best doctor!

GINNY: Disparaging of Western culture? Really? [*Beat.*] Pejorative? No. [*Beat.*] Fine. Questions?

BRIAN [*calling on a student*]: Red shirt. [*Pointing to chart*] Yes, 85% is what it *says*, yes very good, 85%. You are all very good at math. But people, what does it mean?

VALERIE [*to director*]: I'm sorry. Kneel here? At—
              What, is Brutus sick,
      And will he steal out of his wholesome bed,
      To dare . . .
Not at "upon my knees." Really? OK.

[VALERIE *kneels and marks the script.*]

BRIAN: These numbers represent real people who breathe, and work, and fuck, and they don't have time for you to sit in rooms and speculate about the 2% of the 75.3% that when factored into '*a*' equals an aggregate of some bullshit.

[VALERIE *rises and kneels, rises and kneels.*]

GINNY: . . . the findings beg for a contextual framework.

        JACKSON: Context, people.   BRIAN: I'm talking context.

JACKSON: Go look at him. Not his chart. Look at the patient!

GINNY: One subject spoke of the American male's attraction to her "otherness."

VALERIE [*trying different emphases*]: What is *Brutus* sick . . . *What*, is Brutus sick . . . What is Brutus, *sick*? . . .

JACKSON: No, you looked at his insurance status. [*Beat.*] Hell yes. That's exactly what I'm implying.

BRIAN: Be the scientists persecuted for voicing that which is not palatable. What's the most non-palatable conclusion? There is only one. [*Beat.*]

JACKSON: He's a seventy-three-year-old, overweight diabetic with a compromised heart and high blood pressure. [*Beat.*] The toe needed to go.

GINNY: Over and over subjects noted the dominant culture's perception of our subjects as sexually promiscuous, and scholastically dexterous.

JACKSON: Three months' night rotations? Again? [*Beat.*] No. I would not describe myself as a hothead. [*Beat.*] Well then fuck you. [*Beat.*] No. I'm sorry, was that disrespectful? What I meant to say was fuck you.

[JACKSON *exits.*]

BRIAN: I refuse to state it for you. So . . . One more time. [*Pointing to the projections*] . . . We return to the differentials: The stereotype-content model predicts differentiated variables.

[JACKSON *reenters.*]

JACKSON: I can see how that was disrespectful. [*Beat.*] Please accept my apology. Emergency, nights. [*Beat.*] I understand. Thank you.

[JACKSON *exits.*]

[BRIAN *says the following; after his first sentence,* VALERIE *and* GINNY *speak their lines simultaneously as Brian continues, more quietly now. Light lowers on* BRIAN, *as the projections on the wall become blurrier.*]

BRIAN: Incorporating a fundamental friend-foe judgment [*pointing to the graph*] warmth, plus a capability judgment. The SCM proposes that societal groups are appraised as intending either help or harm and as either capable or not of enacting those intentions. The model posits that the combinations of competence and warmth dimensions produce four distinct emotions toward social groups: pride, envy, pity, and disgust. Those subjects able to track the class, physical attractiveness, generational distinctions, etc., in African American subjects tended still to respond . . .

VALERIE: And upon my knees [*kneeling*]—I'm sorry to beat a dead horse, I really do think this is where I should. [*Rising*] And upon my knees . . . So that's . . . uh . . . metaphorical?

[VALERIE *listens, in frustrated earnestness.*]

GINNY: . . . several notable conclusions . . . amongst them, a direct correlation of racist stereotyping to low self-esteem, depression, and anxiety. Not only do these results beg for a more robust examination of mental health care amongst these communities broadly . . .

VALERIE: And upon my knees [*walking awkwardly to her mark*] I charm you, by my once-commended beauty— [*To director*] And I'm still standing? OK. OK, I'll make it work. [*Shaking it out . . . getting her bearings*] Can we start at the top? Is Brutus yes. Is Brutus sick? And is it physical to walk unbraced and suck up the humours of the dank morning? What, is Brutus sick,

GINNY: The work lays a foundation for the debunking of the Western assumption that Asian Americans are immune to the destabilizing effects of institutional and societal . . .

BRIAN [*in silence*]: I do hope you're following this. [*Beat.*] Questions?

[*Lights out.*]

ACT 1

SCENE 1

[*Lights rise on* VALERIE, *leaning against the stage door wall in the back of a theater. She's on break. She wears a short leather jacket over her rehearsal skirt and corset. She speaks to her mother on the phone.*]

VALERIE: . . . Yes . . . I know . . . I've just been busy. I know I said I'd call earlier this week. But we're on the phone now. My bad. [*Beat. Drawing deeply on her cigarette*] No, I'm totally listening. You just said, you said, "the hydrangeas are bigger this year than ever." See Mom, I listen. [*Beat.*] Oh my God . . . you're seriously going back to that? A hungry group of fellow campaign volunteers didn't judge *you* because *I* brought a tuna casserole to a potluck. No ma'am. Tuna casserole carries no cultural or class implications. Seriously, I didn't take a watermelon. [*Long beat.*] I thought we agreed not to talk about the campaign. [*Beat.*] Because of course you should vote for him, and I'll just get annoyed and we'll argue so let's not talk about it . . .

[*She's been interrupted.*]

That's ridiculous. Yes. I know. Kennedy. So, it'd be OK if someone shot Hillary? [*Uncomfortable moment.*] So you think you'll
make it to the show this time? [*Beat.*] Sort of a lead . . . [*exhales*]
Of course I've stopped. No, I know. I promised, so I don't OK.

[*She puts out the cigarette.*]

Look, um, I know I said I'd stop asking, but, I was hoping you
could spot me like just three hundred to get me to the end of the
month. Yes, I know you put me through school. Yes, and graduate school. [*Pause.*] Forty thousand. [*Beat.*] Just a three hundred
dollar loan, until I get paid Friday. [*Beat.*] Yes ma'am. [*Beat.*] Yes
ma'am. [*Beat.*] Yes ma'am. Could, could I talk to Daddy please?

[VALERIE *lights another cigarette.*]

Daddy? Hi. It's Valerie . . .

SCENE 2

[*Lights rise on* GINNY YANG, *sitting at an empty conference room table,
deep in her Blackberry.*]

[BRIAN *enters.*]

GINNY: Good . . . I was beginning to think I had the wrong place.

BRIAN: Committee for the study of minority matriculation, retention,
and recruitment?

GINNY: Someone was very proud of that. [*Beat.*] The meeting is supposed to be here right, twelve thirty, right?

BRIAN: They changed it . . .

GINNY: When? [*Looking through phone*] I didn't get any . . .

BRIAN: Today.

GINNY [*still scrolling*]: I don't think so. I never got a . . . They didn't . . . [*Sees it, showing him*] Oh. They changed it to—

BRIAN AND GINNY: One thirty.

BRIAN: Yes. I think they rescheduled so they wouldn't have to buy us lunch.

GINNY: Well then, you're early.

[GINNY's *always kind of half looking at or typing on her Blackberry.*]

BRIAN: I'm hiding from my research assistants.

[*Beat.* GINNY *doesn't look up . . . she's Blackberrying as though her life depends on it.*]

Does it not strike you as strange?

GINNY: I'm sorry?

BRIAN: I said, doesn't it strike . . .

GINNY [*still only kind of looking up*]: Strike you . . . I got that. Strange what?

BRIAN: Strange, that if they wanted diversity, institutionally, they wouldn't just hire some people of color, right?

GINNY: Absolutely.

[*Surprised agreement yanks her out of her Blackberry.*]

You didn't tell me your name.

BRIAN: Brian. [*Beat.*] White.

GINNY: Ginny—half Chinese, half Japanese.

BRIAN: Brian White.

GINNY: Of course. I see how I did that. [*Beat.*] So your work? [*Back in it.*]

BRIAN: Cognitive neuroscience. When I can get to it. Recently I've spent too much of my time teaching children.

GINNY: Children?

BRIAN: Yes, indeed, at the leading research institution in the world, I'm teaching 101 survey courses to undergrads. It's my penance.

GINNY: What did you do? [*Plunging deeper into her Blackberry*] Wait a minute, oh my God . . . you're that guy.

BRIAN: What?

GINNY: Your op-ed. You started that whole race firestorm.

[*She's impressed.*]

BRIAN: In the flesh.

GINNY: I should have recognized you . . . you're a big deal.

BRIAN: Are you Googling me? In front of me?

GINNY: "White," the race guy, is that your real name?

BRIAN: Yeah. I get that a lot.

GINNY [*still Googling*]: So, cognitive neuroscience . . .

BRIAN: I started in neuropsych . . . [*Beat.*] Or maybe I could just let you—

[BRIAN *gestures toward her Blackberry, where she is still Googling.* GINNY *sets the phone down sheepishly.*]

I started in neuropsych, detoured through biology and sociology, and sort of migrated to neuroscience, where I stayed.

GINNY: Does one really "migrate" to neuroscience?

BRIAN: I did. [*Beat.*] And you're Ginny Yang. Psychology golden girl.

GINNY: I prefer wunderkind. [*Beat.*] How do you know me?

BRIAN: I Googled you. You weren't there. You do Asian stereotyping.

GINNY: Asian *American*. Women. Mostly third generation. So you know me why?

BRIAN [*after a beat*]: I've been criticized for focusing on too narrow a demographic. I was considering broadening . . . my parameters . . . to be more inclusive.

GINNY: Of?

BRIAN: People other than Blacks, Whites, and Latinos.

GINNY: So did you?

BRIAN: Huh?

GINNY: Broaden your racial parameters . . .

BRIAN: No. No, I didn't.

GINNY: Why?

BRIAN: There are too many of you, broadly, Asians. No single social experience to speak of.

GINNY: True.

BRIAN: It was untenable . . .

GINNY: Untenable, or inconvenient?

BRIAN: Untenable.

GINNY: Fair enough. [*Beat.*] Have you done one of these diversity committee things before?

BRIAN: I'm the go-to White guy for these. Because I study race. And of course, because I care . . . And you?

GINNY: I generally decline. I don't know. I'm uncomfortable celebrating my marginalization with other disgruntled marginalized people. It's not my job to make the institution behave appropriately. [*Beat.*] In truth, I lost a bet with a Middle Eastern man in my department. And I'm a twoken. [*Pronounced too-ken.*]

BRIAN: Tooken?

GINNY: Token [*holding up one finger*]. Twoken [*holding up two*]. I proudly represent not one, but two under-represented populations . . .

BRIAN: Under-represented? [*Looking up*] Really? 'Cause, I see your people everywhere . . .

GINNY: Women?

BRIAN: The Asian people—

GINNY: You're mistaken. My "people" mostly frequent the hard sciences.

BRIAN: As do I . . . I can't throw a stone without hitting a . . . [*chuckling, notices that she's not amused*] my politics are such that I can make that joke. [*Beat.*] With people who know me.

GINNY: I'll never know you well enough for that to be funny.

BRIAN: Have dinner with me?

GINNY: No.

BRIAN: I can do that better. *Please* may I take you out for dinner?

GINNY: No.

BRIAN: You're a psychologist—

GINNY: Yes.

BRIAN: Just the book kind, or do you actually shrink heads?

GINNY: I write books, and see clients.

BRIAN: So then you know how vulnerable a man is when asking a woman to dinner?

GINNY: I don't study the science of mating rituals.

BRIAN: Not mating. Just dinner.

GINNY: Hmmm.

BRIAN: I really did like your paper. And I'm not just flattering you because I've insulted you. Repeatedly.

GINNY: Thank you.

BRIAN: And again, if you knew me . . . [Beat.] May I flatter you for just another second . . .

GINNY: If you must.

BRIAN: I like the way you write . . . it's smart, accessible, well argued. It was a good read . . . And there was a picture of you. You photograph well.

GINNY: Thank you. What did your last girlfriend look like? [Beat.] Demographically speaking.

BRIAN: I don't date demographically.

GINNY: Humor me.

BRIAN: Blonde. Pretty. Tall. Sort of old-money, good bone structure . . . Yours?

GINNY: Mine?

BRIAN: Your demographic preferences, in men, if you date men, and that's cool if you don't . . .

GINNY: Generally I don't date. [*Beat.*] Can I see that? [*Gesturing to his iPhone—she fiddles with it.*] How do you . . . [*figuring it out*] oh, here . . . [*keying in something*] That's my number.

BRIAN: OK. Thank you.

GINNY: It's just my number . . . not a promise.

BRIAN: I'll keep that in mind.

SCENE 3

[*Light rises on* VALERIE *sitting on a hospital gurney. She holds a bloody towel to her head . . . she wears a linen rehearsal corset and petticoat, also covered with blood. She sits. The clock ticks. She fumes. Finally:*]

JACKSON: I'm sorry I kept you waiting . . .

VALERIE: Yeah . . . uh huh . . .

JACKSON: They didn't clean this up?

VALERIE: No. No . . . they didn't. Waiting room was empty, and still there I sat, bleeding all over myself for hours . . .

JACKSON: A nurse didn't . . .

VALERIE: No! No one did anything . . . .

JACKSON: I can tell you're angry . . .

VALERIE: Yes . . . Yeah . . . Yes . . . I am, very . . . yes. I've got a hole in my face . . . it's bleeding. That's a problem . . . this is a lot of blood . . . there's a lot of blood here and this is my face . . . my only way

out of a great deal of debt hinges on my face not being perma-
nently jacked up . . .

JACKSON: It's fine . . . hold on.

[JACKSON *exits and reenters quickly with a cart. He pulls pillows out
from below . . .*]

A nurse should have taken care of this . . . Can you lean back,
please? [*Propping pillows behind her*] There . . .

[JACKSON *cleans the wound.*]

VALERIE: Will I get to see a doctor?

JACKSON: I'm sorry?

VALERIE: I get that I don't rate a fricken nurse . . . but might I see a
doctor at some point?

JACKSON: Dr. Jackson Moore.

VALERIE: Oh. Sorry.

JACKSON [*annoyed because it happens*]: It happens . . .

VALERIE: You don't have on a name tag or a white coat or anything . . .
[*Beat.*] Will it need stitches?

JACKSON: Yes.

VALERIE: How many?

JACKSON: It matters?

VALERIE: It's my face . . .

JACKSON: But the number?

VALERIE: Will it scar?

JACKSON: I don't know . . .

VALERIE: The cab driver said five.

JACKSON: Five what?

VALERIE: Stitches.

JACKSON: Oh, well, the cab driver should know.

VALERIE: Please make them nice? And small.

JACKSON: I'm very good at stitches.

VALERIE: It's my face.

JACKSON: I got an A in stitches.

VALERIE: My face is important. I'm an actress.

JACKSON: That's good.

VALERIE: Huh?

JACKSON: Otherwise you'd be one of those weird medieval fair people. And I didn't think we did those . . .

VALERIE: We?

JACKSON: Our people . . .

VALERIE: Oh. No. I'm in a show. Shakespeare.

JACKSON [*laughing*]: I didn't think our people did that either . . .

VALERIE: You should get out more.

JACKSON: So who hit you?

VALERIE: No. No . . . no, I walked into a flat. I explained to the officer in the lobby, I told the woman who checked me in, I told the triage nurse . . . seriously, what does a Black woman have to do to convince you guys that she hasn't been beaten?

JACKSON: Well, the triage nurse has a legal imperative . . . We make her ask . . . I, on the other hand, was just concerned. Most of the heads of pretty young women I have to stitch up got made that way by some jealous asshole . . .

VALERIE: I walked into a flat . . . it's there in those papers [*pointing to charts*] . . .

JACKSON: A flat?

VALERIE: A piece of the set . . . there was a jagged thing . . . a nail maybe and . . .

JACKSON: Seven . . .

VALERIE: . . . it was just very dark and I enter at a run and . . . and it . . . seven?

JACKSON: Stitches . . . I'd guess seven . . . Since you care so much. But I promise to make them small and pretty. When I'm done it'll be almost as though you have a third eyebrow . . . So, no one will even notice the scar . . .

VALERIE: That's supposed to be funny?

[JACKSON *has threaded the needle, brought a lamp close to her face, donned gloves, and is about to sew . . .*]

[JACKSON*'s starting.*]

Wait! Wait! Will it hurt?

JACKSON: Of course.

VALERIE: A lot?

JACKSON: I numbed you up. You'll be fine. I promise.

[*He sews.*]

I do see theater. I saw "Lord Help the Child That's Got His Mama" at the Atrium last fall. And um, "The Brotha's Got a Song to Sang" . . .

VALERIE: Oh . . . well . . .

JACKSON: Yeah. See, this brother was a gang banger and his mama kept prayin' to set him straight, and he accidentally shot his sister, and when he was in prison he got saved and then he found out that it was really the neighborhood drug dealer that killed his sister . . . and they all sang a song, went to church, and lived happily ever after.

VALERIE: Which play was that?

JACKSON: Both . . . You're done. Eight.

VALERIE: You said seven . . .

JACKSON: Sue me. [*Removing gloves*] I'll send someone in with paperwork . . . take four Ibuprofen as soon as you can . . . And try not to walk into any more walls . . . flats.

VALERIE: You're not going to give me any?

JACKSON: Advil? They charge an arm and a leg for those . . . I promise, they'll cost less over the counter. [*Beat.*] I wasn't implying that your abusive drug dealing pimp boyfriend isn't a good provider . . . I just noticed that you don't have insurance . . .

VALERIE: Thanks.

JACKSON: Some friends and I run this neighborhood clinic. It's not the Ritz. But we're good doctors. It's a better place to go for something like this. Well, anyway, we give out free birth control . . .

VALERIE: No, I don't need—

JACKSON: I wasn't—

VALERIE: Of course not . . .

JACKSON: Anyway . . . here's the card . . . I've written my number on the back should you have follow-up questions. About your head. You don't have to go there, but do go to a doctor and have the sutures removed in a week.

VALERIE: OK. Thanks. Sure. Thanks.

[JACKSON *exits.* VALERIE *turns the card over. Lights fade.*]

SCENE 4

[*Light on* BRIAN *in his office area, on the phone, looking at his computer.*]

BRIAN: You're the dean, Steve, of course this is a scold. [*Reading e-mail*] I'm looking at it: "In reference to comments made . . . calling my attention to article 2.b.g of the teacher–student ethics manual. I bring in sooo much research money, and you're sweating me over an undergrad survey course? And never mind why I'm teaching an undergraduate survey course. [*Still reading*] Verbal denigrations? . . . I did not . . . That's what the class is. "The Sociological Implications of Scientific Methodology." [*Beat.*] Yes. I gave them an upbraiding, but I didn't call them stupid racists. OK, I did not call them stupid. This isn't about the class.

[*Light up on* GINNY, *in session with a young woman.* GINNY *sits, clipboard in lap, glasses on. She has compassionate listening down to a science. Scenes alternate.*]

GINNY: We ended your last session with a goal. Right, Akiko? You were to practice clearly stating your opinions to authority figures. And how did that go? In English please, Akiko.

BRIAN: I didn't kick out the students of color. I excused the ones who actually got it. Hold on . . . let me look it up . . .

[BRIAN *begins rifling through his papers.*]

GINNY: You're too hard on yourself. You've definitely made progress. But, is what I think really important?

BRIAN: It's right here. Goldstein, that's Jewish, right. [*Beat.*] Biracial? Really? What and what? Oh. I thought it was a Jewfro. LaTasha Jones. [*Conceding*] OK. Fair enough. [*Beat.*] I have a hundred and twenty-five kids. [*Reading name*] Shwargdagala. [*Beat.*] Jesus. Fine.

GINNY [*taking notes*]: Are you able to know, in the moment of an interaction, that you are having an opposing thought?

BRIAN: So I sent home my three kids of color. Do you not find it problematic that in a survey class of a hundred and twenty-five, there were only three?

GINNY [*rifling through notes*]: I'm hearing you say that it's what you don't say in that moment that makes you anxious.

BRIAN: And this is tragic how?

GINNY: . . . and how does that anxiety feel in your body?

BRIAN: Steve . . . Steve . . . Listen to me. All they had to do was look at the numbers and write a decent argument for an obvious conclusion.

GINNY: English please . . .

BRIAN: To a person . . . well, to a White person, they manipulated the stats to do what felt best to them. [*Beat.*] Racist is not the worse thing you can call a person. Not a person whose behavior is racist.

GINNY: English, Akiko . . .

BRIAN: That's bullshit. Yes it is. Yes it is. Fine, then you're racist. [*Beat.*] Are you OK? Good . . . I thought maybe I'd killed you with the force of my ninja-like word.

[BRIAN *hangs up. Regrets it. Redials.*]

GINNY: Yes . . . a very little bit . . . Not conversationally. Still, I want to remind you that in Japanese, a direct utterance of the word "no," *eee-yeh*, is considered offensive.

BRIAN: Hi, Vicki . . . I lost the signal, could you put me back through to Steve, please . . .

GINNY: If I said to you, is your dress green, and clearly it is not, rather than *eee-yeh*, "no," you would reply *che-gow*, "not quite" or "maybe not" . . .

[*She has been interrupted.*]

It's an example. What others might perceive as submissive or passive is simply a culturally specific way of communicating.

BRIAN: Yeah, I'm still holding.

GINNY [*after a beat*]: "Others," the dominant culture . . . yes, Whites, well anyone, even second- and third-generation Asian Americans, have embraced these values. [*Beat.*] Exactly. And so, to be heard by the dominant culture, how might you state your—

BRIAN: Sorry Steve. Lost you there. I don't think you're racist. Why the e-mail? Clearly, you're documenting . . . Do I need to worry?

GINNY: I'm simply trying to help you build strategies, um, an awareness of certain dynamics.

[*Beat. Do you have problems with authority?*]

Well, sure I . . . I'm sure we all, humans, have struggled with authority on occasion . . . I see we're out of time. Let's keep this in mind for next week.

SCENE 5

[*Lights rise on* VALERIE *in a chair facing out, in* BRIAN's *lab area. She wears a new Obama T-shirt. On her forehead now just a couple of butterfly Band-Aids. A complicated web of electrodes is fastened to her head.* BRIAN, *offstage, speaks into a mic.*]

VALERIE: Are we almost done? The flyer said two hours.

BRIAN: We pay for overtime . . .

VALERIE: It's not that, it's just . . .

BRIAN [*voiceover*]: Could you tilt your head just a bit to the right . . .

[VALERIE *tilts left.*]

BRIAN [*voiceover*]: Right, please.

VALERIE [*adjusting*]: Sorry.

BRIAN [*voiceover*]: And center. [*Beat.*] Great.

[*The lights dim, and a hot white light—a blank projection screen—hits* VALERIE.]

Watch the projection screen. I'll show you some random photographs. Remember, try not to think. We're monitoring your brain's immediate response to visual stimuli . . .

VALERIE: So I shouldn't, like, form the words, in my mind, of what I see as I'm seeing it . . .

BRIAN [*voiceover*]: Please, just take it in . . . OK.

[*Lights dim.* VALERIE *is shown slides projected on the fourth wall. The colors play across her face.*]

VALERIE: OK.

BRIAN [*voiceover*]: As soon as you've seen it, just say "Next" . . .

VALERIE: OK. [*Beat.*] Next.

[*Slide changes.*]

 Next.

[*Slide changes.*]

 Next.

[*Slide changes.*]

 Next.

[*Slide changes.*]

 Next.

[*Slide changes.*]

 Next. No. Wait. [*A moment.*] I know that person.

BRIAN [*voiceover*]: What?

VALERIE: Where did you get these pictures?

BRIAN [*voiceover*]: Damnit.

VALERIE: Yeah, she's an actress.

[*Harsh fluorescent lights go on.* BRIAN *enters, begins to remove electrodes through the following.*]

BRIAN: Well, that's a phenomenal waste of three hours.

VALERIE: What's the problem? She's the only one I recognized. I did a commercial with her last year.

BRIAN: It compromises the control. We hire models. It's easier.

VALERIE: Couldn't we just, like, not mention it . . .

BRIAN: No, we couldn't "like" not mention it. [*Beat.*] Don't worry, you still get paid.

[BRIAN *accidently touches her Band-Aids.*]

VALERIE: Ouch.

BRIAN: Sorry. What happened to your head?

VALERIE: I didn't get hit.

BRIAN: OK.

VALERIE: I'm an actor, so fifty dollars an hour for looking at pictures seems . . . great. And it beats housecleaning.

BRIAN: You clean houses?

VALERIE: Yeah. [*Beat.*] What's your experiment about?

BRIAN: Study.

VALERIE: Fine study.

BRIAN: We're observing neurological responses the brain has to various images. How the brain is affected by race. The most exciting developments right now derive from developments from neuro-science as much as from neuropsychology. It's phenomenal, the rigorous computational analyses of highly defined brain images . . .

[VALERIE *has joined* BRIAN *near the laptop; he points to the screen as he explains.*]

So, that's a brain. OK. [*Beat.*] I look at the way each area lights up depending on what images you're shown. We monitor changes in body chemistry, pupil dilation, adrenaline levels, even the way your blood oxygenates . . . Pretty comprehensive.

VALERIE: What do you want to find?

BRIAN: I want to prove that all Whites are racist.

VALERIE: Wow . . . that's kind of hot when a White guy says that. [*Beat.*] You didn't know that?

BRIAN: Well . . . I guess a few women have . . .

VALERIE: That people are racist.

BRIAN: Yes. My work is more complicated than that. [*Beat.*] You're a student here?

VALERIE: Just graduated. M.F.A. Acting. [*Beat.*] So we're done?

BRIAN: We're done.

VALERIE: Can I put my name on a list or something, so I can do more of these?

BRIAN: I'm not sure how much you'd be called . . . Most of my peers don't use people of color . . . Af . . . Black respondents . . . but I can certainly make sure you're on it. The list.

VALERIE: You're the only one who studies Black people?

BRIAN: No . . . I'm the only one trying to factor in Blacks for control groups and also as respondents. It's a nuanced difference.

VALERIE: Not terribly. White people are more comfortable keeping us *under* the microscope.

BRIAN: Well put. But again, not me . . . [*Beat.*] You don't seem quite the housecleaning type.

VALERIE: You could use someone to help you out around here.

BRIAN: Cleaning?

VALERIE: Sure.

BRIAN: I could probably find some things for you to do . . . I don't know about cleaning. It makes me uncomfortable. Can you do Excel? Do you mind tedious? Sorting, filing . . .

VALERIE: Yes . . . I need six more hours of anything a week to meet my goal.

BRIAN: Your goal.

VALERIE: Rent.

[VALERIE *exits stage right.* BRIAN *watches her go.*]

[*Lights fade.*]

SCENE 6

[*The actors, on phones, stand or sit in different tightly lit areas. Light rises on* BRIAN. *He has dialed. A conventional ring.* GINNY *picks up.*]

GINNY: Hello?

BRIAN: Hi. This is Brian White, calling for Ginny [*beat*] Yang.

GINNY [*visually pleased, vocally neutral*]: Speaking.

BRIAN: Thanks for your number.

GINNY: Again, why were you broadening your parameters?

BRIAN: Good. Thank you. I'm well. And how are you?

GINNY: So, something you said, when we met, you said that you read my work to broaden your racial parameters . . .

BRIAN: I also said that you're attractive—

GINNY: Why, if your data collective was productive, would you . . .

BRIAN: It seemed like the right thing.

GINNY: Right why?

BRIAN: Inclusivity . . .

GINNY: Political correctness?

BRIAN: Because some random public agenda made me feel guilty? No . . . Because science should leave no stone uncovered.

GINNY: Unturned.

BRIAN: Beg your pardon . . .

GINNY: Nothing . . . sorry . . .

BRIAN: So, about my previous offer?

GINNY: Dinner?

BRIAN: Hoping . . .

GINNY: Hold on . . . let me look . . .

[*Lights fade on* BRIAN *and* GINNY, *as* GINNY *scrolls through her phone calendar. Light rises on* VALERIE *dialing. The ring tone is a funky dance groove. Light up on* JACKSON; *he's picked up . . .*]

JACKSON: Jackson . . .

VALERIE: Doctor [*flipping card over*] Moore?

JACKSON: Yes.

VALERIE: Oh . . . Valerie . . . Johnston. I was in the emergency room a few days ago, you gave me your card. The bloody Black girl with the weird clothes . . . [*pause*], and, well, I thought maybe I could make an appointment at your clinic, you, you mentioned your clinic, um, to have the sutures removed . . .

JACKSON: This isn't the clinic number . . .

VALERIE: You wrote this number on the back of the card, so I thought . . .

GINNY AND VALERIE: Are you there?

JACKSON AND BRIAN: Yes . . .

GINNY [*still scrolling through the schedule*]: Hold on . . .

VALERIE: I thought . . .

JACKSON: To set up an appointment you'd need to call the number on the front of the card.

VALERIE: Oh. Sure. OK.

[JACKSON *and* VALERIE'*s lights go out as* VALERIE *hangs up abruptly.*]

GINNY: Sorry about that . . .

BRIAN: Dinner, tomorrow. Six?

GINNY: Oh, I have a client.

BRIAN: Eight?

GINNY: Wednesday?

BRIAN [*looking in his phone*]: Friday, six o'clock?

[*Light up on* VALERIE, *who's dialing again . . .*]

GINNY: No good. I have a symposium.

BRIAN: Saturday, brunch?

[JACKSON'*s phone rings.*]

GINNY: Eh.

BRIAN: Dinner?

GINNY: Yes.

[JACKSON *answers.*]

JACKSON: Jackson . . .

VALERIE: Yeah, I got that.

BRIAN [*to* GINNY]: How about The Harvest. Saturday. Eight.

JACKSON: You got that? . . .

GINNY: OK.

BRIAN: Great.

[*Lights out on* BRIAN *and* GINNY.]

VALERIE: Your name, I got that.

JACKSON: This is . . . ?

VALERIE: I just called you. Valerie.

JACKSON: The clinic takes messages, Nikki's pretty good at getting
    back to you.

VALERIE: You're serious?

JACKSON: The receptionist should call you back . . .

VALERIE: You're trying to make me feel like an asshole?

JACKSON: Beg your pardon?

VALERIE: OK. You wrote your number on the back of the card. Your personal cell phone number. Right?

JACKSON: I'm not following you.

VALERIE: The clinic number's on the front of the card. Of course a reasonable person would know to call that number for an appointment. But I called your cell phone, because you gave me the number. So. Here I am calling you, and you act like you don't remember me? No one doesn't remember me.

JACKSON: Well, Valerie Johnson . . . .

VALERIE: Johnston . . .

JACKSON: Well, Valerie Johnston, had you said, "I think you're a charismatic and interesting person and I'd like to get to know you . . ." we could have proceeded in that vein. You, however, first made reference to your need to schedule an appointment . . .

VALERIE: Do you always talk like that?

JACKSON: Like what?

VALERIE: "You however first made reference to . . ."?

JACKSON: And still, my point . . .

VALERIE: "And still, my point . . ."

JACKSON: I'm beginning to regret giving you the number . . .

VALERIE: I'm beginning to regret calling it.

JACKSON: I wasn't trying to make you feel like an asshole.

VALERIE: Of course not. OK well, I'll call the clinic. Thanks for your help.

JACKSON: Wait.

VALERIE: I'll call the clinic.

[VALERIE *hangs up. Almost immediately her phone rings.*]

Hi Jackson. See how I did that? Because your number pops up here on the screen, and it's the same number I just called.

JACKSON: Despite your abundance of charm, I would like to cook dinner for you.

VALERIE: Because this went so well.

JACKSON: Because that's what I wanted to do when I wrote my number on the card.

[*Lights out.*]

SCENE 7

[*Early morning at* JACKSON'*s clinic. He's on the phone with his brother, and preparing for patients. He hasn't even turned the open sign around. He's hot (mad).*]

JACKSON: I told you not to call me while I'm at work. I don't have time for this . . . [*He's interrupted.*] Listen . . . [*interrupted again*]. No . . . You listen . . . Fine, yeah, it's a sickness . . . you're sick . . . Fine. No. You made your own choices . . . You did not trip and fall on top of a crack pipe. [*Beat.*] Good. I'm glad you're straight now. That's great Harold, I'm very proud of you. I just need for you to hear me clearly. You find a halfway house, you find your last crack ho and shack with her, you live in the fucking subway for all I care, but you will not drag all that craziness into my mama's house.

[GINNY *enters the clinic.* JACKSON*'s back faces the door . . .*]

I will hurt you. I will come to Mama's house and I swear to God I will kill you. I will kill you in front of her and your boy if you bring harm to this family . . . [*Beat.*] You got the money I sent? Yeah, five hundred . . . hey, Harold . . . use it for food.

[JACKSON *sees* GINNY.]

We're not open yet.

GINNY: I'm sorry I . . . your door was . . .

JACKSON: Do you need help?

GINNY: I called yesterday.

JACKSON: Are you unsafe in your home?

GINNY: I don't think so?

JACKSON: Are you here because someone or something makes you feel endangered in your home?

GINNY: Oh God no.

JACKSON: OK. [*Beat.*] I can show you to an examination room . . .

[*Long pause.* GINNY *is waiting for something, and he's confounded.*]

GINNY: . . . Oh . . . No . . . I'm Ginny. You're Dr. Moore? . . . Yes, there it is, on your [*pointing to his name tag, shaking his hand*] . . . It was nice of you to extend yourself, Nicole said to . . . So you read the documents I . . .

JACKSON: You sent literature?

GINNY: Your nurse—

JACKSON: No.

GINNY: Assistant? Nicole—

JACKSON: Nikki.

GINNY: She said —

JACKSON: The receptionist

GINNY: She said that you would have / read

JACKSON: I'm sorry, I would have?

GINNY: To prepare for our discussion—

JACKSON: No. Read? Why? . . .

GINNY: OK. [*Beat.*] I could walk you through it . . . [*Beat, regrouping, digging through bag, handing him a mound of papers*] I spoke with Nicole . . .

JACKSON: Nikki . . .

GINNY: Nikki, last Wednesday. [*Beat.*] This isn't going well.

JACKSON: So, I don't have time to make this a big thing. You can leave your samples on the counter . . . I'm sure someone will get back to you. We could really use XR versions of Saxagliptin, whatever you have.

GINNY: I'm sorry?

JACKSON: Samples. Anything diabetes? . . . [*Beat.*] You're welcome to leave brochures.

GINNY: I don't understand.

JACKSON: You didn't bring samples?

GINNY: I think you think I'm with a pharmaceutical . . . [*Regrouping*] I'm with the study.

JACKSON: Nikki scheduled you?

GINNY: With the University?

JACKSON: The University?

GINNY: Harvard.

JACKSON: Oh, of course. The University. [*Beat.*] So what do you want?

GINNY: Bodies.

JACKSON: We're not a morgue . . .

GINNY: Alive ones. Asians. Specifically your Chinatown traffic? For a study.

JACKSON: We don't do studies.

GINNY: As a policy?

JACKSON: Our patients aren't guinea pigs.

GINNY: I think you misunderstand . . . If you would just read the . . .

JACKSON: No. You University people come in here all the time . . . we're busy here. We're trying to save lives.

GINNY [*looking around—it's a neighborhood storefront clinic*]: If you say so . . .

JACKSON: Unless you're here to offer resources . . .

GINNY: If you could please just read the . . .

JACKSON: So presumptuous.

GINNY: I spoke with the . . . Nikki. Maybe you could just read the . . .

JACKSON: Yeah. I'll be sure to do that.

GINNY: You won't. But you should. Just do. Please. [*Beat. Softening*] Please.

[GINNY *exits.*]

[JACKSON *throws the study into the wastebasket.*]

[*Blackout.*]

SCENE 8

[VALERIE, *on the phone outside a theater, wears a jacket over her costume and now sports a rather impressive Grecian wig. It's getting close to the end of her break.*]

VALERIE [*she's on hold, looking at her watch, drawing deeply on a cigarette butt*]: Yes . . . I'm holding for Emily Rossner, I've been holding for like five minutes . . . our publicist said to call at one fifteen. Valerie Johnston, *Julius Caesar* at Shakespeare Rep. Yes, I'll hold. [*Another long hold. Finally:*] I'm holding for—oh— [*putting out cigarette, jumps to*] . . . Emily, thanks for—

[*Emily has asked the first question. Beat.*]

—I auditioned. [*Beat.*] Umm . . . I auditioned. [*Pause, perplexed*] How did I come to play Portia? . . . Well, I did undergrad at Tish, M.F.A. at . . . oh, OK, you have my bio . . . well, there was a posting on the hotline . . . the equity hotline, and I scheduled an audition and, I auditioned . . . with a monologue from Lady Macbeth . . . you know "screw your courage to . . . ." Oh . . . I hadn't thought of the casting choices as brave. [*Beat.*] I guess, I mean,

I'm young, but I'm told that I have a certain gravitas . . . and I know Portia speaks of having been Brutus's wife for some time, of being older, but this is relative . . . she may have married at twelve . . . [*Pause.*] Oh that . . . OK, well, it's not really color-blind casting, I'm his wife . . . Well, neither are any of the actors actually Roman. Really, it's really just me, an Asian spear-carrier, and a Croatian Gaius Trebonius. [*Beat.*] Conrad's a traditionalist . . . it takes place when it would have taken place . . . realistic design elements, I'm very excited to make my professional debut at Boston Shakes—OK then. Um, thank you for your time . . . if you have any more questions feel free to—

[*The reporter has hung up.*]

SCENE 9

[BRIAN *and* JACKSON *sit on a bench in a locker room. They've been playing basketball. Both are sweaty and winded.*]

JACKSON: Wait, wait . . . what did you say she said?

BRIAN: It wasn't even what she said . . . it was how she said it. It was tone . . . tone. Like . . . like you should be so lucky . . . like coming off of her in waves.

JACKSON: That shit's hot.

BRIAN: What?

JACKSON: Yeah, generally, if "you should be so lucky" is comin' off of the girl it means, "you should be so lucky."

BRIAN: I'm just off my game . . .

JACKSON: You're off your game?

BRIAN: That's funny?

JACKSON: I don't know if you can be off it, if you wasn't ever on it.

BRIAN: I've been on it.

[JACKSON *has wiped himself down, put bottled water on a towel and swabbed at his armpits, and is spraying an aerosol deodorant under his arms . . . then, for good measure, everywhere.* BRIAN *watches.*]

BRIAN: You're going back to work like that?

JACKSON: I have a date . . .

BRIAN: You're not gonna shower?

JACKSON: I don't want to wash off my pheromones. [*Beat.*] So why are you off your game?

BRIAN: I meant at work. The department . . . something's shifting. They're fucking with my money, pulling back my research assistants . . .

JACKSON: But you're the man, right? Aren't you like their golden boy or something? What'd you do?

BRIAN: I'm not like you. I don't *do* things. [*Beat.*] I called a roomful of undergrads racist. Then I called my dean racist. I may have intimated that the institution is racist in an op-ed, and on NPR.

JACKSON: That's funny—

BRIAN: But only to the degree that all historically White institutions are . . .

JACKSON: Oh . . . so, professionally you're almost as self-destructive as I am . . . OK. I'm liking this . . .

BRIAN: Oh no . . . what did you do now?

JACKSON: I cut off a fat old man's toe and then quit, and then begged for my job back.

BRIAN: You did what?

JACKSON: Oh no no no . . . you're the one who fucked up this time. What happened?

BRIAN: They've been throwing money at me to say this stuff for years, you know that. Only now that my numbers are coming in like I knew they would and I can back it up, it's as though they're hearing it for the first time.

JACKSON: Right? They pump you up. You the man . . . then as soon as you take a little initiative . . . boom . . . three months nighttime rotations.

BRIAN: So listen. They've invited me to do this lecture, kind of out of nowhere . . .

JACKSON: Making you sing for your supper . . .

BRIAN: Or atone for my sins . . . I'm definitely being asked to supplicate, but I don't know to whom and I don't know for what reason . . . Anyway, I wondered if you could come . . .

JACKSON: Sure, if I'm not working . . . text me the info. So, you think you're gonna tap that ass?

BRIAN: I don't tap ass . . . I make sweet sweet love to a woman.

JACKSON: Once every five years . . .

BRIAN: Fuck you . . .

[JACKSON *has dressed, zipped up his gym bag, and is about to leave.*]

JACKSON [*on exit, to an amused* BRIAN]: Pheromones.

SCENE 10

[*Lights up on* GINNY *on a small raised platform. Shopping bags are draped over her shoulder: Henri Bendel, Saks, Barneys.*]

GINNY: No. No. She gave me the coupon last week. I spent three hundred seventy-five dollars, and the sales girl gave me . . . hold on.

[GINNY *juggles her bags, digging through her purse for her wallet.*]

Here. Look, here's the receipt. [*Beat.*] Who? I don't know her name? I come in here regularly and spend enough money, that on the rare occasion I'm given a coupon, and am told that I will be able to redeem said coupon, I expect the common courtesy of . . . Yes . . . it does say that it's expired, but I didn't look at it. I was told that it would be honored. I could have used it then, but I ordered the skirt, the skirt that you didn't have in my size and I was told that you would honor this . . .

[*Turning around, to unseen person in line behind her*] Can you back up please. Thank you.

[*Turning back to salesperson*] . . . So . . . I can just leave this here, but wouldn't you really rather have the commission than quibble with me over, let's see, what would that be . . . ten percent of two-fifty . . . . What is that, like twenty-five dollars? See the big picture. You'd lose a regular customer and commission over the twenty-five dollars you think you're saving a company that doesn't give you benefits.

[*Beat—she's won. Her pleasure is evident.*]

Thank you. [*Beat.*] Visa.

SCENE 11

[*In the dark, the muffled, guttural sounds of the final moments of climactic lovemaking. Lights rise on* JACKSON *and* VALERIE *untangling themselves from the couch,* JACKSON'*s pants around one leg,* VALERIE *adjusting her skirt and pulling her panties up. An unbearably long moment of fumbling. Finally:*]

VALERIE: I'm sorry. I lost my train of thought. Where was I?

JACKSON: Housecleaning.

VALERIE: Right. Housecleaning. Well, I used to make about fifteen an hour. But now my rates are as high as thirty-five. You just go in and you do an amazing job . . . little tricks . . . wash the windows, the lightbulbs . . . it just sparkles, and they don't know why. On the fourth week, you tell them you're sorry but you realize you've overbooked. Usually you'll get a raise right there. If they don't they'll call two weeks later, and say "name your price," and I say, well, if I squeeze you in on Tuesday mornings, I'd have to give up a job that pays twenty-five an hour . . . and there it is.

[*Silence. They kiss.*]

I've never done this before.

JACKSON: Really?

VALERIE: On a first date.

JACKSON: Technically, mid first date.

VALERIE: Really, and I'm not just saying that . . . I'm a fourth-date girl . . .

JACKSON: So arbitrary.

VALERIE: I know, right?

JACKSON: I made a peach cobbler, if you'd like dessert.

VALERIE: OK.

[*What felt like cable TV passion has just turned into the heights of weirdness. He tries to pour more wine, bottle's empty.*]

JACKSON: I could get more, but we'd have to switch to red.

VALERIE: Unless you want more . . . But I'm, I'm good.

JACKSON: If you're sure. [*Wanting more*] I have a nice Malbec.

[*Pause.*]

VALERIE: Did your mama teach you to fry fish like that?

JACKSON: My grandmama. She's from Virginia.

VALERIE: Ahhh, that's why greens, cornbread, catfish, and a peach cobbler. How do you eat like that and stay so—? Well, it was delicious.

JACKSON: Thank you. I figured you liked it after your third piece.

VALERIE: Two.

JACKSON: Three. [*A moment.*] I counted. There's nothing hotter than a woman with an appetite. I'm impressed and surprised that you handle a hot-sauce bottle so well . . .

VALERIE: What are you saying? . . .

JACKSON: The real test was when you asked for vinegar for the greens. That's just downright sexy and a little 'hood.

VALERIE: I don't know what that means.

JACKSON: No, just . . .

VALERIE: You were testing me?

JACKSON: Whoa . . . don't get touchy.

VALERIE: You purposely didn't put the hot sauce on the table, to see if I would ask for it?

JACKSON: No . . .

VALERIE: So you just wouldn't expect me to use condiments if I wasn't, how would you say, "down"?

JACKSON: You're a little saddity. I wouldn't have presumed to know your relationship to hot sauce, or vinegar.

VALERIE: Malbec please.

[JACKSON *exits to get wine.* VALERIE *makes halfhearted attempts to restore herself to her original first date unrumpledness.*]

[*Lights up on* GINNY *and* BRIAN, *in a restaurant.*]

BRIAN: And then he said, "Professor White, I just couldn't bring my-self to hand in anything beneath my own standards."

GINNY [*amused*]: Nooo . . .

BRIAN: Really . . . And I said, "Well, that's late." And he proceeds to explain that he is not only a straight-A student, but was third in his class at Exeter. And I said, "Well, this is college. Maybe if you'd cared less about standards and more about deadlines you'd have been first." And he says, "No disrespect intended, Dr. White, but that's utterly out of line."

GINNY: Utterly?

BRIAN: Wait, wait, there's more. He asked me where I went to school, and when I said undergrad Cornell, master's and first doctorate Princeton, and second doctorate Harvard, he said . . . no, no. High school.

GINNY: Oh my God.

BRIAN: And explained that third in a class at Exeter would have been among the first at any public school and most private schools in the country.

GINNY: That's ridiculous.

BRIAN: So I said, "When I went to public high school, they had a name for young men like you . . ."

GINNY: Asshole!

BRIAN: Right.

[*That was* BRIAN's *punchline.*]

Asshole.

GINNY: I miss undergrads, they're cute.

BRIAN: So you don't teach at all?

GINNY: Occasionally—a graduate seminar. Mostly they leave me to my research.

BRIAN [*confessionally*]: I went to Michigan undergrad.

GINNY: Well, that's OK.

BRIAN: I wasn't embarrassed. Just sharing.

GINNY: Of course.

[BRIAN *takes a sip of wine.*]

[*Back to* VAL *and* JACKSON; *he's pouring the wine.*]

JACKSON: Truce please. I cooked.

VALERIE: You know, to a saddity girl, saddity's like fightin' words.

JACKSON: I'm sorry.

VALERIE: When we were kids, my cousins in Detroit called me saddity. But they wouldn't beat me up. They were industrious and would take me out to meet their friends and I'd end up getting my "proper-talkin-she-think-she-White" ass beat. Every time.

JACKSON: They set you up.

VALERIE: Of course they did. And I never saw it coming. [*Beat.*] It's a nice name you have.

JACKSON: It was supposed to be presidential . . .

VALERIE: You must be a great disappointment.

JACKSON: Naw, my mom's very proud. I told her I'd be a surgeon when I was in the fourth grade. So, I applied myself. You?

VALERIE: A great disappointment. Hugely disappointing. But they made their bed. They used to take me to all of these cultural things, the ballet, the orchestra, plays. Not for their undying love of art, but because they wanted to make me someone who could get into an Ivy League and graduate and make money. So, there's tension. It'll be OK when I marry a rich doctor and stop this starving artist thing.

[*That's awkward.*]

JACKSON: I just realized. I have so much work tomorrow . . . we should call it a night.

VALERIE: You didn't just.

JACKSON: No, I didn't. I'm sorry. You're offended.

VALERIE: You dismissed me. I said one stupid thing. You're supposed to just not call me back. Not end the date abruptly, especially after . . .

JACKSON: No really, I'm tired. The curtain just came down. I've been on night shifts in emergency and then going directly to my clinic.

VALERIE [grabbing her coat]: It's fine. I've got an early cleaning job tomorrow.

JACKSON: And I'm still not getting the housecleaning thing.

VALERIE: You don't have to.

JACKSON: Well, you're smart. Seems like your energies could go to something more productive.

VALERIE: I'm an actor.

JACKSON: Why?

VALERIE: Because it's what I do better than anyone else can. It's my contribution . . .

JACKSON: You don't think the housekeeping thing sets us back a little? My grandma and mom cleaned houses so I could go to medical school and make something of the family.

VALERIE: Not to help people?

JACKSON: Say wha?

VALERIE: You went to med school to help people, yes?

JACKSON: And your deft portrayal of Portia empowers our people how?

VALERIE: I volunteer for Obama.

JACKSON: I take bullets out of gangbangers.

VALERIE: What's wrong with you?

JACKSON: I've just never met someone so incredibly well insulated. You volunteer for Obama is your whole Black card?

VALERIE: You didn't ask me for my Black card before you . . .

JACKSON: You didn't tell me that you spread your legs prematurely because I'm a doctor.

VALERIE: So, thank you for dinner.

JACKSON: I can walk you to your car . . .

VALERIE: No, no. I'm good. Thank you. [*Beat.*] Actually, where is the bathroom?

[VALERIE *exits to bathroom.*]

[BRIAN *and* GINNY. *Same date. Later.*]

GINNY: . . . you can't even imagine how few people in psych were studying Asian American anything ten years ago. There was a hole, so I decided to fill it. You?

BRIAN: I try to fill holes whenever I can.

GINNY [*is it a double entendre?*]: You came to this work, why?

BRIAN: I'm not sure. [*Beat.*] You've had a squirrel or something trapped in a wall or vent or something, yeah? You know, at first it's this sort of nonlocalized smell, just unpleasant around the edges . . . it's nagging . . . and maybe you just need to take out the garbage or put a lemon in the disposal . . . so you do, and then you run to whatever meeting or class you're late to. A little later you notice again. It's faint, and maybe you're imagining it. You spray a little Febreze and go about your business. Then one day you get home and it's just . . . foul . . . putrid . . . and you know that something has died in the fucking wall.

GINNY: It's a good metaphor.

BRIAN: Well, I hadn't made it yet.

GINNY: Yeah, I know . . . but I get it . . . racism.

BRIAN: You're really going to have to stop doing that. [*Beat.*] My point. I'm not being altruistic. It smells, and I live here. In neuropsych all I could do was point it out, like you do . . .

GINNY: I don't just . . . I address it . . . in my research, with my clients . . .

BRIAN: Anyway, I did five more years because I wanted the tools to nail that shit down. It's a lot of argument to get your head around . . . Seriously, like trying to work out the space-time continuum in a summer movie. There's always a valid other argument. But I've figured it out . . . and I'm right, and the University's fucking with me.

GINNY: Is it possible you look at it all through too narrow a lens?

BRIAN: Explain?

GINNY: So the work I do . . . Perhaps it's given more . . . room, because I'm not railing against the system that created the circumstances.

BRIAN: By circumstances you mean genocide, slavery, internment?

GINNY: Look, I've identified issues in specific Asian populations— depression, anxiety. I've acknowledged the unfair social [*searching*]—dynamic—

BRIAN: Racism.

GINNY: Do you not get tired of that word? I've pointed out the "dynamic" that feeds the cycle. But I address the cycle. What good does running around screaming slavery and internment do now?

BRIAN: What about the White individuals who made the bullshit that makes the low self-esteem?

GINNY: I'm more concerned with the female Asian American individuals who are just trying to get jobs, date, have decent family lives . . . It is what it is. Why not just give people a better set of tools for navigating it?

BRIAN [*not used to this kind of push-back; it trumps him for a beat, then it's just hot*]: So who do you date? Demographically.

GINNY: I told you I don't date. I just sleep around. But because I'm a slut. Not because I'm Asian.

BRIAN: Then why are we wasting time with all this chitchat?

GINNY: Your earnestness and dogged determination appeal to me somehow.

BRIAN: And I like that you're a slutty accommodationist.

[*Back at* JACKSON's. VALERIE's *gathering her things, putting on her coat.*]

JACKSON: I can make you a plate to take with you?

VALERIE: I'm sorry, I just . . . I have a question. Do guys like you come on to girls like me just to punish us?

JACKSON: I told you. It's been a long day.

VALERIE: Seriously, what did I do to you?

JACKSON: So here's what I do. I'm a surgeon. I've been studying to be a surgeon for the last eight years. That's not including all of the pre-meds in college. And I did well. Straight As. It seems I have a natural proclivity for just about anything I do. You know a residency is a hazing, an endurance test. They put us on these crazy hours in emergency. It's just barfing, blood, crying babies, and boys trying to kill themselves via one another . . . We're supposed to pay our dues for a couple of years and then follow around a real surgeon. Who's supposed to teach me. Except they don't like me. We don't need to waste time deconstructing why the Black guy can't get a decent mentor in Boston—

VALERIE: In America, it's not just Boston . . .

JACKSON: Yeah, OK. So, every now and then I don't feel like being treated like Sambo that day, and I push back, just a little. So today I say . . . "No . . . when I wrote that about that patient on that chart there that you're holding . . . it's because I knew what I was doing . . . and when that nurse came up behind me and called Doctor Whoever-the-fuck to come in and second-guess me, and he decided that I'm stucky and so arbitrarily prescribed some kind of bullshit course of action . . . And now the patient's worse, and you will not pin that on me . . . " It doesn't matter how I say it . . . I'm "angry" and "volatile" and "not good at working with others," so I get written up and have to do the whole fucking bedpan thing again. [*Beat.*] So today, I went to work, to the emergency room and I worked for ten straight hours, then I went to my clinic and worked another six . . . Because someone has to take care of those people . . . And then I made your ass dinner. And you're trippin' because I tease you about hot sauce. I don't have time for that.

VALERIE: So the take away is, you ask a woman over and treat her like shit because you had a bad day at the office? I'm really glad you cleared that up.

[*She exits.*]

SCENE 12

[*Lights up on* GINNY *in a different area. She faces the audience . . . Several shopping bags around her feet, she digs through her wallet.*]

GINNY: But I called earlier today. You were holding a blouse. Like the one in the window. Yang. Ginny Yang. [*Distractedly digging through her purse*] Blue, silk, petite two. [*Beat.*] Well, can you send someone onto the floor to check? [*Turning to other sales girl*] While she's looking . . . If I um, if I make a catalogue purchase and have it shipped directly to the store, I don't have to pay shipping charges, correct?

[GINNY's *phone has rung . . . the call is from a client—she's taking it.*]

[*To salesgirl*] Excuse me . . . could you, I just have to . . .

[GINNY *steps away from the counter, keeping her voice low.*]

Hello, Dr. Yang . . . I'm sorry, this is? . . . Are you in crisis? [*Beat.*] Have you hurt yourself? [*Beat.*] Good. I will meet you at the hospital. Listen to me . . . you are OK. You have done your work, Akiko. You have a lifetime of pain that you are just acknowledging, and it is frightening, overwhelming . . . but this is a breakthrough, and I am very proud of you, and I am here for you. Do you have a friend or neighbor who can drive you? Good. Go to Mass General, ask for Psych. I'll meet you there. Remember to breathe. Inhale three. Hold three. Exhale five. [*Breathes in.*] 2 . . . 3. Hold . . . 2 . . . 3. [*Breathes out.*] 2 . . . 3 . . . 4 . . . 5. I will see you soon.

[*She hangs up and returns to the sales counter—the other sales associate has returned. The dress was not on the floor.*]

So it's not there? Then surely you can take it off of the mannequin, please. [*Beat.*] No no . . . it wasn't a question. Please have her take it off the mannequin. Thank you. [*Beat.*] No worries? Why would I worry? I'd just like my blouse. [*Beat.*] Thank you. [*Beat.*] Cash.

[*She rummages in her purse.*]

SCENE 13

[*Light rises on* VALERIE *auditioning for a role, reading from the script. She's at the climax of ghetto passion.*]

VALERIE [*to table of auditors*]: Hi. I'm Valerie Johnston and I'll be reading for [*looking at her pages*] Shalonda. I left my head-shot with the monitor . . . but if you need one I . . . [*referencing her shoulderbag*] . . . OK then. [*Beginning*] . . . I was lovin' you Lenny. All that time you was lookin' at me, an' I thought you was lookin' into my soul. An' you wasn't seein' me at all. An' I was lookin' at you, an' I knowed you seed somthin'. I knowed there's a man in there, an' I could see him, even if you couldn't. And Mama said, she said, "Naw girl, he don' love you . . . he only love you long as you give him what he need, stay scaret, an' stay under 'is foot." An' I toll. I toll . . .

[VALERIE *has stopped abruptly.*]

[*To casting table*] I toll? [*Working it out*] I toll her . . . I toll . . . OOOHhh . . . OK I told her, OK. An' I toll her she was wrong an' I toll her. I got it, sorry, where should I begin? [*Beat.*] No, I can just start over. I'm so sorry, my agent didn't send the right sides, so I'm reading this cold. I was toll to prepare for Mary, the social worker. Oh . . . I seemed a better fit for this role . . . So my agent did tell you that I have a call at two. I'm doing *Enemy of the People* at the . . . Sure thing . . . From the top then. [*Beat.*] [*Assuming an even higher level of ghetto passion*] I was lovin' you Lenny. All that time you was lookin' at me, an' I thought you was lookin' into my soul. An' I—

. . . Oh, OK. Sure. Thank you . . .

SCENE 14

[BRIAN *stands before a small audience in a small lecture hall. He is dressed more formally than we've ever seen him. His demeanor is slightly more nervous, somewhat more impassioned. This is his swan song.*]

BRIAN: I'd first like to thank the Institute for having me, and I have the pleasure of having in the audience two of my deans, Dean Jankowski, Dean Thompson . . . I won't begin to name the rest of you, I surely could only get in trouble that way . . . but suffice it to say, it's wonderful to see so many of you from so many disciplines . . . No pressure.

[*It's a halfhearted joke, and no one laughs.*]

I will just dive in then.

[*Turning to his paper. Establish slide of dolls from Clark Study. Then projected: families of various ethnicities, comprising various numbers of children, or not, some blended families, some same-gendered couples.*]

Our understanding of prejudice has largely been characterized as simple animosity born of fear and ignorance. We have subscribed relatively narrow parameters to the phenomenon of prejudice . . . Evidence for this can be found in bipolar attitude scales, like-dislike, that measure prejudice . . .

[*A complicated scale appears on the small projection screen behind* BRIAN.]

Economists—

[*An even more complicated chart littered with numbers and arrows.*]

sociologists, and psychologists—

[*A black-and-white photograph of three White dolls and three Black dolls, lying on their backs in a row.*]

We've seen this.

[*He turns screen off, angered by the audience's lack of interest.*]

There was a time when I'd have attributed your eyes rolling up into the back of your heads as a direct correlate to my inability to grab you and hold you. I thought it was the words. How the words "Racism," "Prejudice," "Discrimination" always send us into a collective tailspin, a down spiral of defensiveness, embarrassment, animosity, inadequacy, or rage. I get that. I understand that. Honestly, I almost don't resent that. Just LISTEN! Please.

So what are we to do? How then to approach the explaining of that which both defies and begs for explanation? You, my peers and superiors from the hard sciences would say don't. We are not here to explain, we are here to present. God forbid anything as "subjective" as race touch our precious findings. So the data collective sits there, years and years and hundreds of thousands of dollars spent gathering and aggregating, and it sits there while we bullshit around it. God forbid we're the White people saying the wrong thing. Let's face it, you're afraid that government interests and the big moneyed donors you're in bed with will pull your resources. It's unconscionable. Tragic really—your silencing of truth. This dynamic has held our country hostage since its inception. And you'd rather we not look at it? [*Beat.*] Well I say, grow a pair. Suck it the fuck up. The level of aggressive passivity in this room, in these vocations, in this country, is shameful.

Roll up your sleeves and wade though the muck. We must look at the scientific data and embrace that we, the White people, are implicated. Look [*referring to slides*] . . . numbers, more numbers. [*Beat.*] What's that? Numbers. Cold hard data. I'm speaking your language. I've proven that it's there, in our heads, in our cells, in our fucking blood. A predisposition to hate. We are programmed to distrust and fear those with more melanin. We aren't defective, we just must understand our brains, accept our physiology, and acknowledge the social reality that we so virulently deny.

Godamnit, we are scientists—and so bear the burden of enlightenment and reason.

[*They stare at him unmoved, perplexed, and appalled.*]

Don't we?

Fine then. [*Beat.*]

[BRIAN *turns the projector back on, fast-forwards past families to charts and graphs.*]

So, we'll turn to the stereotype content model. Rosen and Gardner predicts differentiated prejudices between . . .

[*Lights and projections go out abruptly.*]

ACT 2

SCENE 1

[JACKSON *and* BRIAN *sit on a bench . . . they've just finished an intense basketball one-on-one. Both are soaked.* BRIAN *is exhausted.*]

JACKSON: Tell me again. So why did you invite me?

BRIAN: I told you . . . Maybe we could just talk about how I kicked ass on the court. Not once. Not once. But twice. See, White man *can* jump!

JACKSON: Obviously I was off my game . . .

BRIAN: I thought your people could use that shit, like turn it into anger, and burn up the court or something.

JACKSON: My people?

BRIAN: You can't channel years of oppression and beat one middle-aged White guy?

JACKSON: I let you win. [*Beat.*] Seriously though, your shit fucked me up.

BRIAN: I guess I just needed a friendly face.

JACKSON: No. You needed your colleagues to see your Black friend not be offended by your weird work.

BRIAN: That's why I didn't want to just hand you the paper to read.

JACKSON: So this is what all the hubbub's about? And now they're going to decide your fate.

BRIAN: Pretty much.

JACKSON: How have you been talking around the heart of your work for all these years? I thought you were an advocate . . . You know, just acknowledging the presence of a social phenomenon . . . that innocuous shit you pseudoscience people like to do. [*Beat.*] Your numbers are straight?

BRIAN: Yeah . . .

JACKSON: The lab work checks out?

BRIAN: Of course.

JACKSON: Damn.

BRIAN: I know.

JACKSON: I'm not surprised.

BRIAN: I was . . .

JACKSON: Of course you were, you're White.

BRIAN: But I'm . . . evolved . . .

JACKSON: If you're so evolved why were you surprised? Seriously, every time a White person acts like you'd expect a White person to act, well, like *I'd* expect a White person to act, all the White people first are like . . . "I don't believe it, it didn't happen, you must have heard it wrong," then, " Oh, I'm shocked" . . . then, "Get over it Black people, it's not that big a deal, Obama's running for president, and you've got Tiger Woods and Michael Jordan."

BRIAN: Come on, I've got the court reserved for another hour . . .

[JACKSON *has tied his shoes and wiped off his face. He's ready to play.*]

JACKSON: You should take a moment to enjoy the glow of your victory, because I'm about to beat your ass.

BRIAN: There's the anger you were supposed to channel into your game.

JACKSON: So you've proven that Whites have issues with race.

BRIAN: They do.

JACKSON: A revelation.

BRIAN: That's not the revelation . . . I know that . . . We have to be able to see it, right? Someone has to say, conclusively, irrefutably, that it's there, before things can get better. You're a man of science . . . I sort of thought you'd celebrate my genius.

JACKSON [*amused*]: You want me to celebrate your genius? How 'bout I just celebrate my victory when I beat your sorry White ass. You coming?

[JACKSON *tosses the ball to* BRIAN. *He walks off stage right and onto the court.* BRIAN *doesn't follow.*]

[JACKSON *enters again.*]

I thought we were playing.

BRIAN [*pause, he realizes*]: I can't believe you really / have a problem with . . .

JACKSON: / Let's drop it . . .

BRIAN: Just answer me.

JACKSON: What.

BRIAN: Do you have a problem with my work?

JACKSON: That's just stupid. How I'm gon' have a problem with your work?

BRIAN: With the study.

JACKSON: Come on man, naw, it's cool, we still aw-ight . . . It's all cool.

BRIAN: OK. What is this?

JACKSON: You gotta let this shit go man, we cool . . . let's leave it.

BRIAN: What is this? "We cool"? Who did you just turn into? Just say what's on your mind. Please.

[*Pause, as* JACKSON *takes a long drink, screws the cap on, wipes his mouth with his shirt.*]

JACKSON: It's just the preliminary study, right?

BRIAN: Yeah . . . the hard conclusions aren't in yet.

JACKSON: And your whole thing is, you're gonna prove to the White people that they're racist.

BRIAN: I don't say racist—

JACKSON: Sure you do.

BRIAN: On the radio, not in my / study

JACKSON: Also a problem /

BRIAN: But it's there, so—

JACKSON: But you're saying . . .

BRIAN: Yeah. OK.

JACKSON: So . . . the lead on like the *Today Show* will say, "Harvard study proves Whites are biologically racist." I don't know, man, that's a dangerous sound bite. I'm not even sure it's relevant.

BRIAN: Sure it is. Legislation is made on statistics and scientific proof.

JACKSON: You know who was into the mixing of race, biology, and legislation? The Nazis.

BRIAN: You're calling me Mengele?

JACKSON: Of course not . . . but I got your attention.

BRIAN: This is the time. Politically we're poised . . .

JACKSON: *If* he wins. And he couldn't possibly, it's America. [*Pause.*] They did those studies, right? . . . The Clark Study—the one they used to push for integration—the little White and Black dolls. They showed the little Black girls and the little White girls the White doll, right? And then they showed them the Black doll and they asked them which one was prettier, and they all said the little White doll, right?

BRIAN: That's psychologists and sociologists. I'm exposing it at an indisputable neurological level so that—

JACKSON: All I'm saying is—

BRIAN: I'm talking / I'm talking here . . .

JACKSON: I'm listening.

BRIAN: No / you're not—

JACKSON: I'm just saying—

BRIAN: Shut up and let me finish. Jesus. [*Beat.*] Until they see it: the brain scans, the blood work, the proof . . . there's room to think the worst. What would the worst be?

JACKSON: I'm not following you . . .

BRIAN: So back to the Clark Study. [*Beat.*] . . . Our conclusion, right, our liberal-minded conclusion is, the children are repulsed by the Black dolls because of societal messages, right, a cultural valida- tion of a certain beauty standard. For the Black girls it's supposed to be internalized oppression, right? But now . . . just pretend you're not well intentioned and liberal. OK? What else might the conclusion suggest?

[*Pause.* JACKSON *has no idea.*]

That the Black doll *is* ugly. I'm just showing what's already in the brain.

JACKSON: The study doesn't stand up, and I'm a *real* doctor, who makes people well and . . .

BRIAN: That's low . . .

JACKSON: Almost a brain surgeon . . .

BRIAN: Almost . . .

JACKSON: So with all my "edumacation," I'm not getting how just because you see a grown brain react in a certain way, or someone sweats, or blinks, or their blood is slightly more oxygenated . . . how you surmise that that's cellular? Why wouldn't that just prove how early and effectively a racist society imprints?

BRIAN: That's true, *if* the majority of White Americans didn't swear that they haven't a racist thought in their heads. That's the lie.

JACKSON: "White Americans." You're only looking at the White Americans who shop at Whole Foods, worry about their ecologi- cal footprints, and teach their babies sign language.

BRIAN: Blue blood or working class, all the same brain patterns . . . all I'm trying to do is prove that it's there. It's what White Supremacy is predicated upon . . . I'm saying even the most liberal-minded White person thinks, subconsciously, deep down, past where we've been programmed not to say it, truly feels that the Black doll actually *is* not only ugly, but wants to kill our children.

JACKSON: It's not enough.

BRIAN: It's my part.

JACKSON: Is it your part, or your ticket to tenure? [*Beat.*] Isn't what makes us human supposed to be our ability to subvert our impulses, our genetically driven impulses? So we don't walk around fucking all the attractive women . . .

BRIAN: You do . . .

JACKSON: Well . . . shouldn't this study, on which you've based your professional reputation, be about more than that? And, where's the part about what the Black people see? Did it not occur to you that we might have less than ambivalent feelings when presented with scary pictures of White people?

BRIAN: I wanted to work on that.

JACKSON: You wanted to?

BRIAN: That's next. I use Blacks mostly for control groups now. Phase 2 is flipping it . . . you think this is a powder keg?

JACKSON: That's bullshit. You better get on phase 2. Such a trailblazer, then figure that shit out then get back to me about the DNA of racist White people.

BRIAN: You're really bothered by this.

JACKSON: Yeah. Yeah.

BRIAN: Well, so is everyone.

[*Long pause, as they put their towels and clothes into their sports bags.*]

Did you really let me win? Both games?

JACKSON: Look at me.

[*He's a beautiful specimen of athletic Black manliness.*]

What do you think?

[*Lights fade on* BRIAN *and* JACKSON.]

SCENE 2

[*Inside* JACKSON's *clinic. Day.* VALERIE *stands at the front desk . . . she waits for a receptionist . . .*]

[GINNY *bursts in, obviously in a hurry, expecting to do another* JACKSON *study drive-by. She's surprised he's not there. An awkward moment or two. Finally:*]

GINNY: So. Is Dr. Moore here?

VALERIE: I, I don't know, I just got [*here*] . . . . I don't think anyone's—

GINNY: I brought these papers for him.

[GINNY *thrusts the study into* VALERIE's *hands.*]

VALERIE: Oh, I'm not . . .

GINNY: We spoke on the phone.

VALERIE: No.

GINNY: Maybe you could put in a good word for me? Get him to just look at it.

VALERIE: I'm sorry? I don't think it's open. The door was unlocked, but I don't see . . .

GINNY: Oh . . . so, he's told you about me. I'm really not the pain in the ass I'm sure he'd have you think. Nicole. Nikki.

VALERIE: Valerie.

GINNY: No. Ginny.

[*Even more awkwardness.*]

Well, thank you, Nikki. If you could just give him that . . .

[GINNY *exits.* VALERIE *puts the papers on the counter.*]

VALERIE [*shouting timidly*]: Hello?

[VALERIE *is about to exit when* JACKSON *comes in from the back with lunch in a greasy bag . . . something unhealthy from the neighborhood.*]

JACKSON: It was open?

VALERIE: I guess so . . .

JACKSON: Just ran to get my . . .

VALERIE: There was someone here for you . . . Short, Asian woman . . .

JACKSON: That's every other person in this neighborhood.

VALERIE: I've been thinking about something you said the other night . . . about helping our people, or something . . . and first I was like, who the fuck does he think he is . . . And then, I was like, who the

66

fuck does he think he is ... *but,* what do I do ... to further whatever? ... And then I was like "Fuck you" ... to ask me to justify
myself. For being an artist. I really kind of liked you. I did. It's not
very often you meet someone, anyone, who's smart and funny
and quick. I like quick ... and you push back a little ... and that's
nice ... to a point. I really liked that you're Black and handsome
and "articulate."

JACKSON: You like that I'm Black and *articulate?*

VALERIE: There were quotes around [*making air quotes*] "articulate."
[*Awkward beat.*] I'm a "good girl." I'm the girl who went to
church, and kept my virginity until junior year college, and felt
guilty about it after. I'm the girl that pretty much anything I do
or say is just because I'm earnest and honest, and I was never
the girl who knows what not to say and how to be disinterested
enough to get the guys like you. I'm not slick ... and I say the
wrong things.

JACKSON: You couldn't just call?

VALERIE: OK then.

[VALERIE *exits.* JACKSON *picks up the study* GINNY *has left and exits
with it as lights fade out.*]

SCENE 3

[*Light rises on* GINNY, *in session.*]

GINNY: In English please, Akiko. Would you like a tissue? [*Gesturing toward tissue box*] OK. [*Putting the box back and listening*]
That must be very difficult for you. [*Listens.*] You've never had
your marginalization named? [*Listens.*] Marginalized. Made to
feel small. Made to feel, outside. [*Listens.*] Oh, you've never been

marginalized. Because you consider yourself White. [*Beat.*] I didn't . . . OK. Well, certainly identity is subjective. [*Listens.*] I'm not sure that what I think matters. [*Beat.*] Is it important to *you* that I agree? [*Listens.*] No . . . No, I wonder only why you might have chosen me? [*Beat.*] Do you think of me as White? [*Beat.*] Identity is tricky. Um hmmm. Um hmmm.

[GINNY *takes notes.*]

[*To patient:*] It sounds like you just want respect. And what would that look like?

[*Lights up on* VALERIE *sitting on the floor in* BRIAN's *lab. She sorts and stacks 5 × 7 cards. She makes stacks of different categories on the floor. Placing each card in its own pile as she sorts. The sound of her putting the cards on the floor is audible, like a loud game of cards.* BRIAN *works on the computer.*]

VALERIE: White. White. White. White. White. Asian. White. African American. White. White. White.

BRIAN: Do you have to do it out loud?

VALERIE: White. White. White. White . . . .

[*He shoots her a look. She sorts a little more quietly.*]

[*In* GINNY's *office:*]

GINNY: So it's complicated. We've talked about this before, Akiko. [*Beat.*] Yes, I strongly identify as Asian American. But that is my choice. No . . . No, I wonder only why you might have chosen me though?

[GINNY *listens aggressively to her patient.*]

[*Back to* BRIAN's *office:*]

VALERIE: White. White. White. African American. Other. White. Other. Latino. African American. African American. Other.

[*To* BRIAN:] Who's other if you don't use Asians . . . ?

BRIAN: Native American, biracial, African-Caribbean, Middle Eastern . . . some Jews don't like to mark White.

VALERIE: Seems like you'd rather be "something" than "other."

[*In* GINNY's *office:*]

GINNY: I see. You think of me as White. [*Beat.*] Identity is tricky. Um hm. Um hm. It's complicated. So yes, again, I strongly identify as Asian American. But that is *my* choice. [*Beat.*] It is not necessary that we identify similarly. [*Subtly frustrated.*] We're set then for the same time next week? Great. Consider my question though. What would make you feel "seen"?

[*Light out on* GINNY. *In* BRIAN's *office:*]

VALERIE: Don't you have grad students who could do this?

BRIAN: No. [*Beat.*] Val. It is not economically efficient for me to pay *you* to not let *me* work.

VALERIE: Sorry. [*She sorts quietly, then*] You said you would canvass with me this weekend.

BRIAN: Yeah . . . I got buried here.

VALERIE: Well, you can imagine how much fun New Hampshire was for me. [*Beat.*] Do you even want him to win?

BRIAN: Do they brainwash you guys down there at headquarters?

VALERIE: It won't happen without everyone—

BRIAN: Valerie, it won't happen.

VALERIE: Then I don't know why you're doing this work.

BRIAN: I'm not. Because you won't stop talking.

[VALERIE *goes back to her sorting. She picks up a new stack.*]

VALERIE: White. White. White. White. White. White. Other. White. [*Beat.*] Do you keep track of the race of the person surveying?

BRIAN: Why.

VALERIE: Obviously this stack belongs to a White person.

BRIAN: Valerie, why are you fucking with me today?

VALERIE: I read your study.

BRIAN: You too?

VALERIE: It scared me . . . can I tell you why?

BRIAN: Yeah, sure, I'm happy for you to have an opinion about that which you know nothing. It's great that you feel empowered to weigh in on this work I've been doing for decades because your skin is brown. I get it all the time. Do you know Blacks at the med school coalesced with Blacks in Af-Am and Anthropology to petition me to stop my work?

VALERIE: Why?

BRIAN: Because "the mingling of science and race could prove damaging." You're here now because when my department got pushback, I lost my funding and they pulled my research assistants. They're shaming me into leaving.

VALERIE: You think it's hard studying Black? Try being Black.

BRIAN: Of course I get that. I'm just tired of having to say "I get that" all the time.

[BRIAN *looks at* VALERIE, *turns silently and goes back to his computer, slightly defeated, highly frustrated.* VALERIE *stares. Finally she begins picking up the cards, stacking them neatly in a box. After too long of this,* BRIAN *crosses to* VALERIE, *sits next to her.*]

Listen Val, I'm just a White guy who wanted to know what it meant, in my brain, to be a White guy. I just wanted to compare what your crazy public-minister people are always screaming about with what's happening in my head . . . and when I started to look into the heads of people who look like me, even I was shocked . . . so then I wanted to know what people who looked like you saw . . . when they see the things that I see. And that we see two different worlds, is blowin' my mind. And I'm wrong to want to explore that? It's E equals MC squared. It's Darwin, and Galileo, and Newton, and Copernicus . . . And what do I get? Shut down by someone like you? What the hell do Black anthropologists and economists know about science? What do you know about science? Life is so hard for you why? You're beautiful? You clean houses 'cause you think it's cute and it pisses off your mother? And you're gonna criticize me for trying to make tangible that which your people are accused of making up?

VALERIE: It's more complicated.

BRIAN: I'm sure it is.

VALERIE: It's complicated.

[VALERIE *reaches out and touches* BRIAN's *face. It startles them both. He covers her hand with his. The moment is almost more . . . then a mutual agreement to let it pass.*]

[*Light fades, and* VALERIE *continues sorting, as* BRIAN *returns to the glow of his computer. Sound of typing accompanies.*]

VALERIE: White. White. White. White. Other. White. White. White. White . . . [*Pause.*] Hey, Brian?

BRIAN: What?

VALERIE: I do believe I heard you call me pretty.

BRIAN: I said beautiful.

[*The glow of* BRIAN*'s computer is the last thing we see.*]

SCENE 4

[GINNY *rushes up as* JACKSON *is pulling the curtain closed on an emergency room much like the one he met* VALERIE *in.* GINNY *almost bumps into him, not yet seeing him.*]

GINNY: I'm sorry. I'm looking for a patient, um, Hayashida, Akiko Hayashida.

JACKSON: A patient?

GINNY: The front desk told me . . . Oh, it's you.

JACKSON: You have patients? Here?

GINNY: We met at your clinic. Ginny Yang.

JACKSON: I have a very good memory. But you have patients here?

GINNY: I try not to. I got a call from Psych that a client of mine . . .

JACKSON: You're a doctor.

GINNY: If you'd read my study . . . the proposal . . . You know what, I just need to find Akiko . . .

JACKSON: They took her up to Psych, it'll take them a while to check her in. She's fine, superficial wounds. She wanted attention.

GINNY [*starting to leave*]: Well, she got it. This is her second time here.

JACKSON: Wait. Please. I did read your study. [*Beat.*] You wouldn't give up.

GINNY: Then you know I'm a real doctor.

JACKSON: Well. [*Not really*] I didn't realize you were going to provide free counseling.

GINNY: You didn't give me a chance to tell you . . .

JACKSON: I was busy. Saving lives. Who's doing the head shrinking?

GINNY: Counseling. It matters, why?

JACKSON: I don't want a bunch of twenty-four-year-old White girls brushing up their psychiatric-doctoring skills on my patients.

GINNY: I'll do it.

JACKSON: OK, then.

GINNY: You're welcome.

JACKSON: You're welcome.

GINNY: OK, then.

[JACKSON *exits.* GINNY *watches, then heads off in the other direction.*]

SCENE 5

[VALERIE *wears an Obama hat, jacket, and T-shirt. She holds a clipboard and a stack of brochures. She stands in a very tight, square light. She's waiting for someone to answer the door. When the door is opened the quality of the light changes.*]

VALERIE: Good afternoon. My name is Valerie Johnst . . .

[*The door is slammed shut. Another square of light appears. She goes to it.*]

Hello. My name is Valerie Johnston and I wondered if you are registered to vote, and wanted to tell you a bit about my candidate . . . Barack O—

[*The door is slammed. Another light.*]

I wondered if you're registered to vote. My candidate, B—

[*The door is slammed. Another light.*]

Hi. I'm Valerie Johnston. [*Pointing to pin, pleased because they noticed*] Yes. Obama. [*"It's nice that you're volunteering your time."*] Thank you. You have no idea how mean people can be. [*"Oh I do."*] Right. [*Beat.*] Well you know, change doesn't happen unless we all . . . [*"Where were you when Hillary needed your support?"*] I'm sorry? [*"Did you canvass for Hillary?"*] I'm sure Hillary could be a fine leader. But . . . Well, I . . . she's not my candidate. [*Beat.*] Yes, I am a feminist . . . but she's not my candidate. [*Beat.*] The first woman president would be incredible. As would the first . . . [*Beat.*] So I'm guessing you don't need brochures. [*Beat.*] Well, it's really not about gender or race . . . he's the best candidate . . . Yes . . . I am deeply aware of gender disparity . . . But some of us have . . . [*Beat.*] . . . You know what . . . why don't you spare us both and just slam your door in my . . .

[*The door slams. Light out.*]

SCENE 6

[GINNY *sits on the edge of the bed, barefoot, buttoning up her blouse.* BRIAN *has entered, in pajama bottoms, with a glass of water for* GINNY.]

GINNY: I bought out of all my classes for the fall . . .

BRIAN: You're beautiful . . .

GINNY: But this spring I'm teaching one, which will kill me. I'll never make my deadlines. I've got two book deadlines, a journal review, and I'm supposed to be presenting at A-Psy next month . . .

BRIAN: I just want to point out that this, this is really sexy. This post-coital banter of yours . . .

GINNY: I'm sorry. [*Beat.*] It was really nice. You should know about me that I've been criticized for being un-nurturing.

BRIAN: Are you?

GINNY: Nurturing is for babies and plants.

BRIAN: That's hot.

[*He kisses her, eases her back down onto the bed. It seems that the shirt might be coming off. Shirt is not coming off.*]

GINNY: I've really gotta go or I won't be any good tomorrow.

BRIAN: Arrrrggggghhhhhhhh. OK. [*Beat.*] You're the youngest tenured person in the universe, why can't you stay with your boyfriend for one night?

GINNY: I work harder *because* I have tenure. [*Beat.*] Boyfriend? Really? Already? OK. Sure. I guess. Seriously, tenure just turned up the pressure.

BRIAN: Why?

GINNY: I don't know . . . I have to prove that I deserve it.

BRIAN: Prove . . . ?

GINNY: What do you want me to say?

BRIAN: I guess I thought maybe you'd say you work so hard for the girls . . .

GINNY: What girls?

BRIAN: The girls you study, the girls you counsel.

GINNY: I counsel women.

BRIAN [*after a beat*]: I'm just saying . . . all the hoops you jumped through . . . and you have it, you have everything . . . why keep jumping? Just be still in the success for a second.

GINNY: Sit still?

BRIAN: I'm just trying to give perspective. Why don't you stay over?

GINNY: I don't do that.

BRIAN: I won't give you a key. You can take your toothbrush with you . . . I just thought maybe we could, you know, talk some sexy data analysis, go another round and then spoon?

GINNY: I don't spoon. I don't even use that word.

BRIAN: Why are you here?

GINNY: You're the first man I've met lately who doesn't seem deeply infected with yellow fever, you're attractive, seem to be passionate about doing good in the world, and you're the smartest person I know who isn't me. [*Beat.*] But I really do have to go.

[*She puts on her shoes, begins to gather her things through the following.*]

BRIAN: No. You cannot go. It's eleven forty-five. If you do not go home and work, the world will not end.

GINNY: I just gave you great sex, decent conversation. You're such a leech.

BRIAN: I gave you great sex . . .

GINNY: I concede that.

BRIAN: What is this thing that you do?

GINNY: I'm going.

BRIAN: Just talk to me. Don't go home and order a new pair of shoes.

[GINNY *gasps audibly.*]

Yeah. I see you. That's an abnormal amount of shopping that you do. That, my dear, is a problem.

GINNY: We're talking about my shopping habits because I wouldn't stay and spoon?

BRIAN: We're talking about your shopping habits because I think you think you're perfect. And you're not.

GINNY: You're jealous.

BRIAN: I'm horny.

GINNY: I have to go. I have work to do.

BRIAN: I'm sorry, that was uncalled for. I just . . . It would be nice to make enough money to one day support your shopping addiction. [*Beat.*] Forgive me for sounding like a Neanderthal, my mother was a feminist—she raised me better than this, but listen, I want to take care of you a little bit. I want for you to know, that I've got you . . . Stop proving and just lean into me for a second . . . Relax into me . . .

GINNY: Relax? Relax into you? Are you kidding me? I have to show up and represent. Do you know how many people are lined up behind me to take that shit away? You're supposed to know that, but you don't because it's . . . untenable . . .

BRIAN: I've always understood that. How would you not know that I've always understood that? It's what my career is built on. It's what I do! You know that!

GINNY: So what, you want an award!

BRIAN: Yes. Why should I not want an award? That's good business. That's access to people and money . . . that's influence. That's legislation. Yeah, I want a Balzan and a Templeton, and yes, I want a Genius Grant too.

GINNY: It's not even called that anymore.

BRIAN: I want a Genius Grant.

GINNY: A Genius Grant will not make your dick longer. I don't know why I said that. I like your dick. Your dick is long enough.

[*Long moment.*]

BRIAN: I want a Genius Grant.

GINNY: I don't think you do. People around you get weird, hostile sometimes almost. My mother actually said, "Oh, she's such a genius, but she can't find a man and give me grandchildren." I went out with this guy who after sex turned to me and said, "So that's what a power fuck feels like." I was doing my work, for the girls as you say, and the more White men said "good job," the further away I got from what I thought I was doing. Praise is insidious and seductive, and I hate it. So you don't talk to me about what you don't know. Just sit there in the want of it. But shut up about what you don't have.

BRIAN: You love it. You love the power.

GINNY: What's wrong with you?

BRIAN: I'm just saying, who does a person have to fuck to get a Genius Grant around here?

[GINNY *reflexively raises her hand to slap him, catches herself, and then:*]

GINNY: OK, OK. [*In exaggerated Chinese accent*] I likee White man longa longa penis. It very, how do you say, it very very please me.

[GINNY *pushes* BRIAN *onto the edge of the bed. Kneels in front of him. It is disturbing. It should be. She has unzipped his pants. It takes him a moment to understand what's happening.*]

BRIAN: What? . . . Stop . . .

GINNY: Why you no hard? I not please?

BRIAN [*intending "stop"*]: Ginny . . .

GINNY: I make White man feel good and feel good and feel good.

[GINNY, *back to audience, begins to fellate him.*]

So, you tell Ginny if I no please.

[*Images of the faces the audience saw at the top of the play wash across the stage. They cover every surface; they are huge and vibrant. They are all the audience can see.* BRIAN *and* GINNY *recede into the images. In darkness we hear* BRIAN *enjoying it despite himself.*]

[*Just silence, darkness, and then one image after another.*]

[*Lights out.*]

SCENE 7

[*Night.* JACKSON *stands next to a back alley stage door.* VALERIE *enters.*]

JACKSON: . . . truly, magnificent.

VALERIE: I wouldn't have expected you to come.

JACKSON: You sent me an e-mail.

VALERIE: I sent everyone in my address book an e-mail.

JACKSON: You're luminous.

VALERIE: I don't understand you.

JACKSON: Really. I liked the play, a lot. But every time you walked out there, the whole stage lit up.

VALERIE: Thank you.

JACKSON: I'm sorry I didn't see you in *Julius Caesar*.

VALERIE: It was nice of you to come.

JACKSON: I'm sure you have people to get to?

VALERIE: No, my people came opening night.

JACKSON: Look . . . I'm sorry about . . .

VALERIE: Oh no no no. Not necessary. [*Beat.*] I actually had a moment . . . when I thought I might owe you an apology, that's why I stopped by the . . . It passed. You—stir me up.

JACKSON: Can I take you to get a drink or something?

VALERIE: No.

[*Pause.*]

JACKSON: It's an interesting play.

VALERIE: I know. Right?

JACKSON: And nobody's mama was on crack.

VALERIE: Nope. No crack in Ibsen.

JACKSON: Could we try again. Maybe dinner?

VALERIE: I told my girlfriends about you. There's some debate as to whether you're a sociopath, or just a horrible person.

JACKSON: OK then. Good luck with your life.

VALERIE: I really do appreciate that you came.

[VALERIE *exits.*]

SCENE 8

[BRIAN *sits at a table in a restaurant. He has been waiting for some time. Finally* GINNY *sweeps in.*]

GINNY: A dissertation defense ran late . . . I should have called . . .

BRIAN: Yes.

GINNY: I'm sure you thought I wasn't [*going to come*] . . .

BRIAN: Yes.

GINNY [*silence*]: I should have called you back . . . How was your week?

BRIAN: Two weeks, Ginny. [*Beat.*] I've had better. Yours?

GINNY: Busy.

BRIAN: Of course.

GINNY: When we first met, you joked about the prevalence of my people in the sciences . . .

BRIAN: *We* joked . . . [*Beat.*] . . . You just said, "*you* joked," you laughed too, that's *we* . . .

GINNY: They don't give us tenure, Brian . . . Asian American women, our tenure rate is seriously something like none to every twenty White guys. [*Beat.*] Brian, I don't do self-reflective, you know that.

BRIAN: I've yet to meet a psychologist who does.

GINNY: So I have this client . . . this girl at the clinic . . . she came in today. Couldn't be more than seventeen. And she's so smart. Just really . . . could have the world. She's not particularly pretty, but Asian goes a long way. Ooo, I heard myself say that. You know what she does? She comes home from school and does her homework and then does the books and schedules for her family's business. She's up until two A.M., every night. And she's not going to get out, Brian. None of these "Harvard Asians" are from her world, our world . . . most of us never get out. She'll work those books, and her brother will inherit the business, and she'll marry and have kids, and they won't get out of Chinatown either. She says, "I don't really have problems, but you give me a Barnes and Noble's gift card if I come for six weeks, right? . . ." And we sit and stare at one another, and sometimes, just because she feels sorry for me, she tells me about a test that she's nervous about, or something. And today I gave her a big stack of twenty-dollar gift cards, and suggested she exfoliate her forehead every now and then and to always use condoms, and gave her my blessing. [*Beat.*] I shouldn't have run away, huh. I don't do girlfriend well. I've never actually done girlfriend.

BRIAN: That's fine. But I do want you to know . . . that I was properly chastised. Your punishment was diabolically effective. I tortured

myself. I looked good and hard and long at the White male patri-
archal asshole you'd proven me to be. I had the existential crisis
you hoped for. But then you know what? I realized that *I* got off.
What did you get out of it?

GINNY: The satisfaction of a job well done?

BRIAN: We'll never be close enough for that to be funny. [*Beat.*] I'm
sorry.

GINNY: OK.

BRIAN: [*Beat.*] Ginny, you don't say "I'm sorry." That's not un-
nurturing, that's just not nice.

GINNY: I'm sorry.

BRIAN: Thank you.

GINNY: Can you be OK with it that I'm better at everything than
you?

BRIAN: Can you try to be nice?

GINNY: Yes.

BRIAN: Then I will endeavor to. Can we please go home and make-up
spoon?

SCENE 9

[JACKSON, *at the hospital, speaks to an angry superior.*]

JACKSON: Yes, sir. But I'm doing twice the rounds. [*Beat.*] Yes . . . I understand that. [*Beat.*] There's a file folder, right there, behind the
nurses' station, that says, "resident rescheduling requests". . . Yes
. . . and I filled it out fully expecting that a superior would say yes
or no. And you're getting on me just for filling it out? [*Beat.*] I've

never asked for a . . . I've never been late . . . never missed a day
. . . I just needed to pick my brother up from the . . . All you had
to do was say yes or no. But you're reprimanding me? For asking.
I don't know what this is?

[*And then, in a long beat,* JACKSON *sees it all very clearly.*]

You want to break me. You want me to lose my mind trying to
rationalize why you might want me broken. You are pathologi-
cally committed to seeing me fail. But not just fail . . . you want
my soul dead. [*Beat.*] You want to kill my soul. But I get it now. I
can't heal people when my soul is broken. My soul must be intact
for me to do my work. [*Beat.*] Please feel free to tell yourself and
your colleagues that you have won, if that's what you need to do.
Because I'm out . . .

SCENE 10

[*It is 2008.* BRIAN, JACKSON, *and* GINNY *are mid-meal. There's an un-
touched place setting. A long time passes as the men on either side of*
GINNY *watch her text. For* JACKSON *it's amusing . . . for* BRIAN, *beyond
annoying.*]

GINNY [*finally noticing the men*]: I'm sorry, guys. Just one thing . . . I
   didn't send, I think I composed, but didn't . . .

BRIAN: What if you didn't hit send . . . would, would the world end do
   you think?

GINNY: Shit . . . . OK . . . Here we go . . . There it is. OK.

[GINNY *makes a grand gesture of hitting send, and is satisfied by the
whoosh. She lays the phone facedown. She's back.*]

OK. [*Long pause.*] I'm sorry.

JACKSON: No hide off my back. This is great . . .

GINNY: Brian did the chicken.

JACKSON: It's good.

BRIAN: Thank you. Well, next time we invite you over . . . maybe
Ginny will actually put her phone down for five minutes . . .

GINNY: I'm totally present. [*Beat.*] Are you offended, Jackson?

JACKSON: No. It's bad manners, but I'm not offended.

[BRIAN's *phone has been docked on a speaker on the credenza. It
rings . . . he pointedly doesn't get it . . . the ringing stops, the music
continues.*]

BRIAN: Look at what just happened. It rang. I didn't answer. It stopped
ringing and we're all OK.

[JACKSON *looks uncomfortable.*]

GINNY: Are you sure you gave your girl Friday the right time?

BRIAN: Yes. [*Beat.*] Shit . . . that would have been her.

[GINNY's *phone rings. She tries not to, but is physically incapable of
not looking.*]

GINNY: Oh, it's . . .

[*She answers.*]

Hey. So you got the waivers? That's great! . . . [*Seeing* BRIAN's
face] Listen . . . I'm going to need to call you back.

[GINNY *hangs up.*]

[*The doorbell rings.*]

BRIAN: Good. Here she is . . . I'll . . .

[*He leaves to get her.*]

JACKSON [*to* GINNY]: She's late. I already don't like her.

GINNY: You don't have to like her. I don't think it was a set-up.

JACKSON: Of course it was.

GINNY: Well, I don't even know her. But I really don't think it was a set-up. [*Beat.*] I get the impression you're doing OK for yourself.

[VALERIE *enters, followed by* BRIAN; *she walks straight to* GINNY *without seeing* JACKSON.]

VALERIE: I am so sorry I'm late.

GINNY: It's nice to meet you.

VAL: Likewise.

GINNY AND VALERIE [*to* BRIAN]: She's pretty.

GINNY: Nikki . . .

[VALERIE *sees* JACKSON.]

VALERIE: Oh my God . . . Really? [*To* BRIAN] Really.

BRIAN: What? So, Jackson, Valerie, Valerie, Jackson. Valerie, Ginny . . .

GINNY: Valerie?

JACKSON: Valerie Johnston.

BRIAN: You two have met?

JACKSON: On several occasions.

VALERIE [to JACKSON]: So you orchestrated this?

JACKSON: Don't flatter yourself. I had no idea.

BRIAN: That's "Angry-Girl"? Valerie? [Beat.] Oh. [Beat.] Ohhh.

VALERIE: Seriously? [Beat.] It's like that fucking Kevin Bacon game.

GINNY: What?

VALERIE [remembering her manners, pulls a bottle of wine from her bag]: Oh God, I do have manners. Here, I brought this.

GINNY: Thank you. I don't know what the Kevin Bacon game is, and I don't understand how your name isn't Nikki. We met at Jackson's clinic, right?

VALERIE: Oh . . . Oh . . . right . . . Well, it's good to see you again. [Beat.] Brian, your house is beautiful. I'm so sorry I'm late . . . I had a rehearsal in New York, then I couldn't get a cab [throwing JACKSON a look, he returns it with a "yeah" shrug], so of course I missed my train . . .

BRIAN: Wait, you're in a show? In New York? And you didn't tell me?

VALERIE [embarrassed]: Schenectady.

BRIAN: Schenectady?

VALERIE: I can put New York on my résumé.

BRIAN: Wouldn't people in the real New York know?

VALERIE: Do I try to tell you about racist brains?

GINNY: She has a point.

BRIAN: Well, but, she does . . . you do . . . all the time.

[*They're all standing around awkwardly. They all look at* BRIAN *as though someone has died.*]

JACKSON: So . . . how you doin' man?

VALERIE: Oh yeah. How are you holding up, Brian? Really.

BRIAN [*to* VALERIE]: You saw me yesterday. People, no one died. Why don't you guys sit down? Here Val, let me heat up a plate for you. [*To* VALERIE] Wine?

VALERIE: Red. Do you have a nice Malbec?

JACKSON: Really man, how you doin'?

BRIAN: I'm fine. I'm fine.

[BRIAN *exits with the empty plate.*]

VALERIE [*to* GINNY]: How is he doing?

JACKSON [*to* GINNY]: Is he OK?

GINNY: Well, it sucks.

VALERIE: He just told me to show up for a pity party. I assumed it was a set-up. What happened?

JACKSON: I just saw him a few days ago . . . he didn't say anything.

GINNY: He's not been talking about it. A couple of weeks ago the dean summoned him. He thought he'd get his usual slap on the wrist, for something he said somewhere . . . they do that . . . he and the dean, it's part of their dynamic . . . But instead he gets "the talk."

[BRIAN *returns with* VALERIE's *plate.*]

BRIAN [*handing plate to* VALERIE]: Oh, you're providing context for the evening's festivities.

VALERIE [*taking the plate*]: Thanks.

BRIAN: [*to* VALERIE *and* JACKSON] Ginny thinks I'm depressed.

GINNY: I didn't say that . . . I just thought you could use a little cheering up.

VALERIE: It would be OK to be depressed.

BRIAN: I'm not depressed, I'm pissed off.

VALERIE: Anger is the flip side of depression. [*Beat.*] My therapist told me that.

JACKSON: You have a therapist? OK.

BRIAN: Yeah, so the dean calls me in . . . and there's this guy I haven't met before . . . and he's introduced to me, I don't remember what his name is . . . it doesn't matter . . . He's their legal counsel. And I should've known then, but I didn't know . . .

VALERIE: He fired you? They do that? They just fire you?

GINNY: In academia it's more like, "We should talk about your prospects here," and they deny you tenure and don't renew your contract. Your colleagues are actually legally bound not to talk to you about it, to avoid litigation, so no one says anything . . . not even good morning. You're shunned.

BRIAN: This time last year, I'm sitting in the dean's office and he's telling me that he's never seen anyone for whom the tenure process would just be perfunctory.

JACKSON: Like you was in like Flynn man.

VALERIE: In like Flynn?

GINNY: He really was their golden boy.

BRIAN: It turned on a dime.

VALERIE: When?

BRIAN: When they knew I was right. What did they think, that I was a hobbyist? They loved it when I went rogue. I'd be like . . . Harvard's racist . . . and they'd be like . . . oh say it some more baby . . . and I'd be like . . . Harvard is entrenched in historical racism and they'd be like, now hit it from the back.

[*Uncomfortable beat.*]

VALERIE [*searching for something to say*]: So, Ginny, Brian tells me you study Chinese people? . . .

JACKSON: Yeah . . . she's exploiting the poor girls at my clinic.

VALERIE: Wait, you and Jackson work together? So Kevin Bacon.

BRIAN [*to* VALERIE]: She's doing a study with some girls there.

GINNY: Women. [*To* VALERIE] They're Chinese, they're short. [*Referring to* BRIAN *and* JACKSON] They get confused. I'm sorry, can we back up? There's a game about Kevin Bacon?

VALERIE: Theater game . . .

JACKSON: Or drinking game . . .

VALERIE: Six degrees of separation . . .

BRIAN: Premise being, every actor is six roles away from a movie with Kevin Bacon in it.

GINNY: Why?

BRIAN: Because in the small spaces between inevitable disappointment and despair humans have to occupy themselves with something, why not Kevin Bacon?

JACKSON: Listen Brian, I've been thinking about it . . . you're an amazing scholar.

BRIAN: Are we doing this? Please don't . . .

JACKSON: No no. No smoke. I know I give you shit . . . but really, I'm proud of you man.

VALERIE: Hey Brian, look over here . . . [*To* GINNY] I'm going to distract him. Look over here, Brian . . . see . . . I'm going to jolt you out of your funk . . . Ready?

BRIAN [*almost pacified*]: Yes, Val. I'm ready.

VALERIE: Admit that this was a set-up. You were so totally setting us up.

JACKSON: Yep. I called that too.

VALERIE: Right? White people are always setting me up with their only other Black friend.

BRIAN: You're not my only Black friend, Jackson. [*To* VALERIE] He's not. [*Beat.*] He's my only friend.

VALERIE: I'm your friend.

JACKSON: Awwww.

VALERIE: It's kind of sweet. Did you think maybe he would be the guy I'd spend my life with, because he has melanin too?

BRIAN: Hey Valerie, look over here. Why don't you have any Black friends?

GINNY: Brian . . .

BRIAN: What? She doesn't. [*Beat.*] Do you?

VALERIE: Not really. I want to. I try.

GINNY: Well, you have Jackson now.

VALERIE: Yeah. No. But I do try to only date Black men.

GINNY: Why?

VALERIE: Because they're hot.

GINNY: Yeah.

BRIAN: I can hear you.

VALERIE: I'm sorry Brian, was that emasculating? [*To* GINNY] Did I emasculate him?

GINNY [*to* JACKSON]: Jackson, I hope we didn't make you feel objectified . . .

JACKSON: It's cool. But Brian . . . I just want you to know, we're here for you man . . . What do you need from us?

BRIAN: I'll get another gig. Of course I'll get another gig. Stanford will take me in a second . . . and I can be that liberal White guy bumping my head against the conservative agenda, feeling really good about myself and misunderstood and nothing will change.

VALERIE: You know it's what you study.

GINNY: She's right. They hate you for what you study. You tell a bunch of liberal-minded, kindhearted, soft intellectuals that they're racist.

VALERIE: By nature it's fucked up . . .

JACKSON: Let me paint a picture. [*Beat.*] So, you're this White guy on the selection committee of some big grant or fellowship.

BRIAN: Let's make it the MacArthur. [*To* VALERIE] That's the Genius Grant . . .

JACKSON: So, you're White, on the decision-making committee. It's morning, you've just poured the coffee into the travel mug, you've said good-bye, maybe to your Black wife or Latino husband, or your Asian lover, or you've kissed your adopted little

Senegalese baby on the cheek . . . and you come to the meeting, with all of your colleagues, half of whom reached forty-five and decided to become parents and so have cute little babies who look like Ginny.

VALERIE: That's racist.

GINNY: But true.

JACKSON: They love those babies. More than they knew they could love anything, right? . . . So, there you are, Mr. Down-with-the-environment-up-with-diversity-I'm-a-good-guy-guy. You open a folder, and the study you're supposed to consider giving an award to says that your brain, your chemistry, registers Black as repulsive. And you're gonna give that an award?

GINNY: I told him that . . .

VALERIE: You know what it is? It's like you've been turned into a Black man. [*To* JACKSON] Right? It's like they're treating him like he's Black.

JACKSON: Here he is, charismatic, intelligent, articulate . . .

VALERIE [*to* BRIAN]: You are very articulate. [*Beat. To* JACKSON *and* GINNY] I told him that. [*To* BRIAN] I told you that.

JACKSON: Pretty soon you won't even be able to get a cab.

VALERIE: Like a Black man. And you start to think, maybe it's me? That's why you're so upset. You're thinking maybe they're right. Maybe I've wasted all of this time. And you're feeling a little crazy, right?

JACKSON: You're feeling like, I played by the rules . . . I played it better . . . My ideas are valid, I'm articulate, I'm attractive . . . so why does no one hear me? They're treating you like you're a nigger . . .

BRIAN: They're supposed to hear me.

GINNY: Why?

BRIAN: You don't understand. They're supposed to hear me.

VALERIE: Why?

BRIAN: Because.

VALERIE: Because?

JACKSON: I know what he's going to say . . .

BRIAN: Because I'm the White guy.

[*Long beat. It lands.*]

JACKSON: And there it is. [*Beat.*] So I realize you're a little down . . . So you know what I'm gonna do . . . I'm gonna choose to believe that you didn't just say, "Because I'm the White guy." Yeah . . . I'm gonna believe that because you're "evolved" you didn't just have some sort of existential White boy crisis because your White privilege didn't work out that day . . .

BRIAN: Shut up.

VALERIE: Brian.

JACKSON: Shut up? You just said shut up to me? Dude, I had shit I could be doing. I'm just here to make you feel better.

GINNY: Everyone's here to support you. Don't do this, Brian.

VALERIE: See, we should have just called this an election party. You can't celebrate a termination.

BRIAN: My thought too.

GINNY: I was trying to be nurturing.

BRIAN: See . . . about these things . . . you all will always trump me. And it's fine . . . I can take it . . . 'cause I'm the guy who gets it.

But just be me for a second. And pretend that you did grow up around people of color . . . That there has never been some big mystique or a great deal of White guilt . . . just enough proximity to see it . . . and an early desire to fix it, this shit we live in. So I devote my life to trying to work that shit out. And I do. [*Beat.*] Wait . . . let's just give me the benefit of the doubt . . . since none of you actually do data analysis or make stereotype content models, or can read brain scans—

JACKSON: Well, I can . . .

BRIAN: My point. I've proven it. I set out with a hypothesis, I followed protocols, and I fucking proved something monumental. [*Beat.*] So what I meant when I said, "I'm the White guy," is that I'm the White guy at Harvard. Who do people listen to? Whose press releases get read and written about in the *New York Times*? Who's the first person they call when something vaguely smelling of whatever happens? The White guy from Harvard. The White guy from Harvard has an inherited platform. And I've got the numbers and I'm right . . . and everyone knows it . . . And I get, from them all . . . shut up. You're threatening our inheritance, our carefully constructed world of entitlement. We have the power to silence you . . . Because your shit blows it all up in our faces. And God forbid White liberals are forced to look long and hard at themselves . . . God forbid they see it.

JACKSON: But you know it's a mindfuck.

BRIAN: But the mindfuck isn't the racism . . . the mindfuck is how dexterous my people are at seeing it selectively. If I'm a redneck, I don't hate you because I'm racist . . . I hate you because you took my jobs and my status. If I'm a White liberal—I don't hate you . . . I sort of pity you . . . but I don't hate you . . . I just don't really want you to live in my neighborhood. In fact, I want to move into yours and make you move out . . . so I can build a Trader Joe's. I am so not racist . . . that I'll let a handful of the best of your children go to my child's school . . . I'm not racist . . . I don't notice that everyone at my job is White. In fact, I'm so not racist that I've been virulently critiquing that for years . . . I'm so So SO not racist. Just please don't fuck my daughter . . .

[*Pause.*]

GINNY: I just think you make it hard on yourself.

BRIAN: Sweetie, I know you mean well . . . you can't possibly . . .

JACKSON: I get where you're coming from, Brian. I've been there . . . and then I realized, sometimes you're gonna get treated like a nigga, and you refocus, put your energies where they're most needed, and fight the battle from a different angle . . .

BRIAN: We've got nothing in common, Jackson. You didn't get treated like a . . .

JACKSON: Like a what mothafucka . . .

BRIAN: You didn't get treated like a . . .

[BRIAN *knows he can't say it and not get punched.*]

. . . you got treated like a man who couldn't listen to authority. And then you quit!!! You did that, to yourself, over and over again. You got treated like the hotheaded Black man with a chip on his shoulder that you are. I got treated like a nigger.

JACKSON: Have you lost your mind? [*To* VALERIE] He has lost his fucking . . .

[JACKSON *gets up as if to leave*—]

BRIAN: Wait, hold on—I'm so sick of hearing preternaturally beautiful people, with intelligence and financial viability, bitch about their lot. You know what? Life sucks. All around. For us all, unilaterally, life sucks. Only White people have nothing else upon which to pin it. Every fucking thing that happens to us is our own poor judgment and bad luck. [*Beat.*] So all y'all motherfuckers can kiss my White ass.

[*He stands, begins to exit.*]

[*Turning around*] And another thing . . . it's not the end of the world to be exoticized, Ginny . . . like it's some fucking curse to be someone who everyone wants to fuck . . .

[BRIAN *begins his exit. The next line is thrown away just as he's off:*]

And the Genius Grant is stupid.

[*He exits. Pause. Pause. Pause. Pause. Pause. Finally:*]

VALERIE: Good luck with that, Ginny.

[*Beat.*]

JACKSON: What makes me crazy is that he has the luxury to let this shit explode his head. Who the fuck gets to go into a tirade because race in America is a mindfuck? Do you get to melt down because you get treated like shit several times a day?

VALERIE: No.

JACKSON: Do you, Ginny?

GINNY: I'm sorry, what? Oh . . . were you talking to me? I'm part of this conversation? 'Cause I was happy to just sit over here in the corner with the Latinos and some Middle Easterners and the handful of Native Americans left. I was happy to just sit here and watch your conversation about race. Because it's just Black and White. So, I'll just sit here and let you all work that out.

[*A moment while it lands. And then it lands hard.*]

VALERIE: Wow. [*Beat.*] We do that, don't we?

GINNY: Yeah, you do. But it's cool. Margarita Perez, Andalah Aboud, Rise with the Fricken Moon Youngblood, and I will just sit over here and exchange shocking anecdotes about nail salons, airport security, and I don't know . . . genocide.

[BRIAN *returns, continuing to remove the plates from the table.*]

VALERIE [*handing plate to* BRIAN]: Thank you . . .

[BRIAN *exits to kitchen.*]

VALERIE [*long beat . . . almost a pause*]: So how did you meet Jackson, Ginny?

GINNY: I went into his clinic and he assumed I'd been beaten.

VALERIE: Yeah, me too, at the hospital . . . The nurse gave me the, "Are you safe in your home . . . ?" and I was like, last time I checked. It took like five minutes to understand what they were asking, which I guess is nice, that they were concerned. Then Jackson wants to know who beat me. And I'm playing that out in my mind, and I think, did they really think that some man was like, "Yo, bitch, put on that Elizabethan costume and get over here so I can beat your ass . . . ."

JACKSON: There's not a damn thing funny 'bout domestic violence.

[*They are all sobered. Because indeed, domestic violence is no joking matter. Long guilt pause.*]

GINNY: Jackson. Do you see how you do that? Two politically conscious liberals were enjoying a moment of irreverent levity and you shat on it.

VALERIE: It is totally a power play. You can always turn a room with "That's not funny." Watch . . . "Hey Ginny, did you hear the one about the about the priest, the prostitute, and the paraplegic?"

GINNY: That's not funny.

VALERIE: See. Now you feel very bad, right? Because you kinda wanted to hear the joke. [*Beat.*] There's no joke. That would be sick.

JACKSON [*to* VALERIE]: You gon' need a ride, Val?

VALERIE [*to* JACKSON]: Sure, I guess. Thanks.

[BRIAN *has returned with dessert on a tray. Little individual trifles or some such.*]

BRIAN: Wait, don't go. Hey Ginny, do the Thanksgiving thing . . .

[*Beat.* GINNY's *not feeling it.*]

Go on . . . do it.

[*It's their story, told so many times it's almost scripted.*]

GINNY: Maybe we should just . . .

BRIAN: Seriously, she does the best impersonation of my sister . . .

GINNY: What are you doing?

JACKSON: If she doesn't want to . . .

BRIAN: Just tell the goddamned story. Please.

VALERIE: Yeah, Jackson, I'll get my coat.

GINNY: It was right before dinner . . .

BRIAN: We haven't even carved the turkey . . .

GINNY: And they just keep razzing her . . .

BRIAN: Razzing?

GINNY: They're just picking and picking . . . You haven't met Brian's sister, have you . . . ?

BRIAN: It doesn't matter . . .

VALERIE: The one with the kid?

JACKSON [to VALERIE]: I need to go . . .

VALERIE: Let her finish . . . And then I do have to go . . . I have to catch an early flight . . . I have an audition in LA . . .

GINNY: OK. So there we are, like Norman Rockwell, except Jimmy's literally bouncing off the walls . . . I thought it was a saying, but this boy's ricocheting off of the walls and you just know that something disastrous is about to happen . . . And Brian's mother's telling Brian's dad to just say the prayer . . .

BRIAN: And Dad's saying, "Not until the boy actually sits down at the table . . ."

GINNY: And Mariam's just sitting there. And now Jimmy's crawling under the table . . . [To JACKSON and VALERIE] He has PDD-NOS . . .

VALERIE: Is that a real thing?

BRIAN: Somewhere between ADHD, Asperger's, and hell . . . He's just so smart and sweet and weird . . .

GINNY: So Mariam puts her napkin down, and she stands up . . .

BRIAN: Here it comes . . .

GINNY [*affecting the slanted shoulders and drawn face of one who is beaten down by the challenges of motherhood and a critical extended family*]: I just want to say, before we eat, that if anyone else has something to say about my parenting, they can kiss my ass. Because Aunt Rachel could stand to lose forty pounds, Uncle Walter is on his fourth vodka gimlet, and Susie has always been a bitch. And I don't comment on any of those things.

[*Whatever was "off" has not dissipated. Another moment.*]

Shit. Dessert.

BRIAN: I should help . . .

[BRIAN *doesn't move.* GINNY *jumps up.*]

GINNY [*to* BRIAN]: You always make me do that.

[*She exits to the kitchen,* VALERIE *joining her, clearing whatever is left on the table.*]

VALERIE: Here, let me . . .

[BRIAN *hands her his plate.* VALERIE *exits.*]

[JACKSON *and* BRIAN *sit in silence for a long time.*]

BRIAN: I know I've heard every one of you say to me, in various ways, at one time or another . . . "What the fuck is wrong with your people?" . . . We were right there with that [*indicating eye to eye*], weren't we?

JACKSON: I thought we were.

[JACKSON *gets up to leave, meaning it this time.*]

BRIAN: I'm sorry. I was completely out of line with the Black man, chip on your shoulder shit.

JACKSON: So out of line.

BRIAN: I do see how fucked up that was.

JACKSON: Good.

[*Stony silence.*]

[VALERIE *and* GINNY *enter with dessert dishes and coffee, before* JACKSON *answers.*]

Val, do you still want a ride?

[VALERIE *collects her things.*]

VALERIE: So thank you, Ginny, Brian. It was a lovely evening.

[JACKSON *and* VALERIE *leave.*]

[GINNY *begins to eat her dessert, while* BRIAN *starts to clear the table. Finally:*]

BRIAN: All I'm trying to say is —

GINNY: Don't.

[*Lights out.*]

EPILOGUE

JANUARY 20, 2009

[*Everyone in his or her separate area.*]

[BRIAN *is scruffy, deeply concentrated . . . he sits on a sofa, surrounded by boxes and lab equipment. He's covered in electrodes, with his finger in an oxygen meter, syringes and vials of blood on a tray next to him. He's hooked up to a portable EEG. He looks at a small television, its back to the audience.*]

[GINNY *is on her couch, comfortably ensconced in a cashmere throw. She drinks coffee and half watches television, half thumbs through a Restoration Hardware catalog. She is on the phone with* VALERIE, *reporting events of Obama's inauguration.*]

GINNY [*on phone*]: Oh my God. It's yellow. A nod to Jackie, but with a flare.

[*Light rises on* VALERIE, *who is on the phone with* GINNY. *She now sports the long, well-maintained—not cheap—weave requisite for all TV ingénues. She wears a well-tailored shearling coat, matching hat, expensive winter boots. She could be a starlet on a Macy's float.*]

She holds an American flag and a Starbucks cup. She faces the audience, fighting the crush of an unseen crowd, far away from the video monitors.]

GINNY: No. It's green. [*Beat.*] Chartreuse.

VALERIE [*shouting*]: I can barely see a screen . . . Can you hear me?

GINNY: I thought you had fancy "I'm-on-a-TV-show" tickets.

VALERIE: I'm in the back of the barely fancy C-list standing only area. It's like a mile away from the B+ list. I thought chartreuse was pink?

GINNY: They're coming out of the church, getting into cars. Can you hear me? I should call you from a landline.

[BRIAN *fiddles with nobs and buttons on his machines. The energy and concentration of a scientist on the edge of his most important discovery.* BRIAN *looks at screens, makes notes, types on his laptop. Searches his arm for a vein.*]

VALERIE: No, no, no. Don't hang up. I wish you were here! Unbelievable.

GINNY [*back to TV*]: Oh my God, she's so beautiful.

VALERIE: Has he come out?

GINNY: Yeah. You know, he looks like he always does.

VALERIE: Sooo handsome.

[BRIAN *makes a fist, finds a vein, ties on a band . . . searches again for the best vein. It's hard to find, maybe he switches arms.*]

GINNY: Just beautiful. The whole family. The girls are so cute . . .

VALERIE: It's so fucking cold.

GINNY: . . . little coats. Oh my God. They're getting in the car.

VALERIE: Seriously, freezing my ass off.

GINNY: What are you doing?

VALERIE: Looking at the back of Rue McClanahan's and Bea Arthur's heads.

GINNY: Michelle's mom's getting into the car. She's going to take care of the girls. God. Why didn't I come with you? His sister's there, with her family. Oh my god, his family's like the fucking United Nations.

VALERIE: It's audacious.

[BRIAN *draws blood. He turns on the EEG, paper starts to scroll out.*]

GINNY: It's exciting.

VALERIE: It's so exciting! It's cold. And exciting!

GINNY: I wish I were there.

VALERIE: Then we'd both be cold and not knowing what's going on. But it doesn't matter it's so / exciting.

GINNY: It's so what? So what? Valerie?

[VALERIE *has lost her signal. They speak their lines at the same time.*]

VALERIE: Hello. Hello? Damn. Ginny? [*To person next to her*] Can you get a signal? GINNY?!! GIN! I'll call you back. I'll call you back, Ginny. [*To person on other side*] Can you get a signal?

GINNY: So what? Did I lose you. Valerie? Valerie? Valerie? Maybe you can hear me . . . Damn it. Valerie?! Val? If you can hear me, call me back, OK?

[VALERIE's *light goes out abruptly.*]

[*The familiar custom ring tone of* JACKSON's *phone brings up his apartment.* JACKSON *watches television as he prepares for work.*]

JACKSON: Yes, Ma. I'm watching. Really. I see. I see. Of course I'm excited. Yes. Ma, are you crying? [*Beat.*] But you're OK? [*Beat.*] OK, I know. I know. Me too. [*Beat.*] No, I get it. It could have been me. No, I'm moved . . . seriously . . . I'm just trying to get to the clinic.

[*He stares at the TV, keys in hand, frozen.*]

Don't cry . . . Awww, Ma, don't cry.

[GINNY's *phone rings.*]

GINNY: Val?

[VALERIE's *light is back on.*]

VALERIE: This is it.

[BRIAN *turns up the volume on his TV.*]

[*The audience hears the sound of President Obama being sworn in. They all take it in. The lights take a long fade on* VALERIE, JACKSON, *and* GINNY, *leaving* BRIAN *alone with his couch, and machines, and boxes.*]

[*Eventually only* BRIAN *is lit by the light of his television screen. Sound of EEG machine ticking. Sound of the president being sworn in.* BRIAN *sits. Watches. The printout from the EEG flows from the machine like ticker tape. It prints and prints and prints.*]